KINGDOM COME!

Our Father in heaven,
thy name be hallowed;
thy kingdom come,
thy will be done,
on earth as in heaven.

Matthew 6:9f., NEB

KINGDOM COME!

by
ROBERT S. PAUL

William B. Eerdmans Publishing Company
Grand Rapids, Michigan

Library of Congress Cataloging in Publication Data

Paul, Robert S
    Kingdom come!

    Includes bibliographical references.
    1. Christianity—20th century. I. Title.
BR121.2.P33   209' .04   74-607
ISBN 0-8028-1564-2

The material in Chapter III appeared in a slightly different form,
under the title "Violent Revolution is Obsolete," in *Presbyterian Life*,
January 1, 1970. Used by permission.

The prayer by Rose-Marie Barth on p. 87 is also used by permission.

Dedicated to

TIMOTHY, LYDIA and MARTIN,
who will probably wonder why

CONTENTS

PREFACE

My younger son, with all the frankness of a teen-ager, said that he thought that it was "stupid," and I can see his point. I had been writing a book about the doctrine of the church (*The Church in Search of Its Self*, Eerdmans, 1972), but had arrived at a point where I could go no further. How could I justify spending time on such an abstruse subject when the world around us seemed to be sick with a sickness near to death? This book is the result of time taken out of the major study, and my son thought it was stupid to write a book about why I was writing a book.

It does sound rather silly when you put it like that. But I am sure he will not think that the concern out of which it sprang is silly. The present time speaks to us all in the imperative mood, and it is partly to answer the unspoken questions of Tim, Lydia, and Martin that it had to be written. In a sense it is their father's *apologia pro vita sua*, at least during the past decade.

The following pages are rather liberally scattered with quotations from Peter Taylor Forsyth, and although I might have chosen other writers — Karl Barth or Reinhold Niebuhr, for example — I chose Forsyth deliberately because he speaks to me with a special pertinence at this time. Also, Forsyth spoke out of an

9

Anglo-Saxon context and out of a Free Church experience that gave him a peculiar ability to discern the theological weaknesses of our time and place. Furthermore, he developed no system and promoted no "school"; he was not anxious to prove himself either orthodox or heterodox; and he wrote as a preacher rather than as a theologian. He allows us simply to judge his words by the gospel, and this enables us to listen to him as a prophet of God's judgment and grace. If you have not met him before, or if he is one of those former friends whom you knew long ago but dropped for more exotic company, let me introduce Peter Taylor Forsyth — but beyond him the one whom Forsyth acknowledged to be at the center of his thought. And through Him, let me introduce again the community committed to proclaim reconciliation.

Pittsburgh, Pennsylvania   Robert S. Paul

No Immunity from Judgment

Europe today is rapidly moving to where antiquity had come, to moral exhaustion, and to the pessimism into which natural optimism swings when the stress and burden are extreme. Do you think that the situation is to be saved by the spontaneous resources of human nature, or the entrance upon the Weltpolitik of a mighty young people like America? Is there no paganism in America? What is to save America from her own colossal power, energy, self-confidence and preoccupation with the world? . . . A Christianity which places in the centre not merely Christ but the Cross and its Redemption, in a far more ethical way than America is doing; a Christianity which is not only set in the presence of Christ's person but caught in the motion of Christ's work, which is not only with Christ but in Him by a total moral and social salvation.

— P.T. Forsyth,
Positive Preaching and the Modern Mind (1907)

Why bother with the church when the world is being torn apart? The question presented itself to me with sudden urgency during a small denominational consultation in which about a dozen of us had met to discuss the nature of the church and its ministry and to ask why

11

the church was becoming irrelevant to so many of its former members.

One side of the small conference room was composed of a large picture window overlooking St. Louis airport, and outside the sky had darkened with the rapid approach of an electric storm. We were beginning our work with a brief service of worship, and from time to time the words of our leader were punctuated by a battery of lightning bolts and the crash of thunder. We listened to the words of Scripture and we watched the storm. It provided an interesting commentary.

You could dismiss us and our little conference at several levels of irrelevance. We were secure, certain that despite all that was going on outside we were in no danger of getting hurt or even wet. Yet what we were doing was a matter of complete indifference to the other people in the hotel, gathered in their own little furnished boxes and absorbed in their own conferences for business or more intimate purposes. We were irrelevant to the world beyond—to the traffic on the freeway, its headlights piercing the storm, intent on getting somewhere fast, or to the planes temporarily grounded, impatiently waiting for the storm to pass in order to get there even faster. And finally there was the Olympian unconcern of the storm itself, swept by impersonal forces in our direction.

The storm is upon us, and it seems to be totally indifferent to what we have been discussing in the church or the plans we have been making for ecclesiastical preservation. A comparatively short time ago we might have been tempted to make some theological capital out of the presence of that storm, to have spoken grandly about the relentless ways of Providence pursuing its own divine ends and forcing even man's proudest technology to pause before it. We might have assumed that the church could rest securely in its special relationship with the Power behind the course of history. Not any more. No special amnesty can be expected, for we recognize within the ominous signs a judgment on the churches' failure to be the church of Jesus Christ.

* * *

To clarify this point let us use an illustration from the earlier history of the church in this century. When I first visited the United States in 1951 I was immediately struck by the similarity between the "free church" situation as it was then in America and that of the English Free Churches as it had been during the first decade of this century.

This was particularly noticeable not only in the unprecedented popularity and affluence they enjoyed, but still more in the casual assumption that this would continue indefinitely. In order to make the parallel clear, it should be said that at the beginning of this century the English Free Churches were at the height of their power and prestige. English Nonconformity embraced all those Protestant churches not in communion with the Church of England; and, conscious of their new strength, they were beginning to refer to themselves by the more positive appellation, "the Free Churches." Politically and socially they were closely aligned with the Liberal Party.

In 1906 the Liberal Party won the election and was returned to Westminster with the largest majority ever seen by the House of Commons. It was resounding testimony that the Free Churches had reached the peak of their influence and popularity. During the previous century they had won the hard fight for their political franchise, and they had already begun to use this to get rid of their remaining social disabilities.[1] Through the effectiveness of their pulpits and by aggressive evangelism at the turn of the century, they found themselves

13

with more influence on popular opinion and public events than at any time since Cromwell and the Puritans. Moreover, they had arrived at this point at the very height of Britain's wealth and influence as a world power.

The earlier exclusion of their brightest and most ambitious minds from the English universities[2] had given them an extremely strong position in trade and industry, and the "Protestant Ethic" had done the rest: in the first decade of the twentieth century the Free Churches enjoyed increasing wealth and popularity, and the prospect seemed to extend indefinitely into the future.

Some of the lay merchant princes were enlightened employers or concerned Christian philanthropists, but many retained the grimmer features of the Protestant ethic long after giving up any vital connection with Protestant churchmanship.[3] Although there were socially conscious groups in the Free Churches that were beginning to support the small Labour Party, the great majority of Nonconformists supported political liberalism, and the *laissez-faire* capitalism of their class and nation. They were in favor of individual enterprise and free trade in church relations and economics, in merchandise and ideas. This led them naturally to support the separation of church and state, affirming that the state should be "neutral with respect to all churches, inasmuch as the establishment of any church by the State is inconsistent with the true Church idea, is an indirect assault upon other churches, and is an obstacle to that 'free and open encounter' whereby alone the truth can come to its own."[4]

Furthermore, the Free Churches had taken a decided step into theological liberalism. The skepticism most of them showed toward the creeds of the Anglican Church encouraged their radical approach to theology; and by the end of the nineteenth century, under the impact of the new science and historical criticism, most of the leaders had broken with their traditional theological systems. R. J. Campbell's "New Theology" was essentially a Nonconformist movement, although he ended in the Church of England.

The significance of this was that the Free Churches felt they held the key to the future. They were demonstrating a remarkable vitality in creating new ecclesiastical societies and institutions for foreign missions, home evangelism, ecumenism (within limits), and many forms of social service. A genuine social concern sent many of the more radical ministers and laymen into the ranks of the Labour Party, and there has been a persistent drift of Free Church radicals from the middle-class centralities of Liberalism into intellectual Socialism. It gave British Socialism a distinctively moralistic flavor. Malcolm Muggeridge's description of his father provides us with an excellent illustration: "My father would certainly have described himself as an essentially religious man. Like many early supporters of the Labour Party, he had come in via the chapel, and his mental attitude continued to the end of his life to bear strong traces of nonconformity — in his case Congregationalism. . . . He was most at home with moral issues — a self-indulgence I have inherited."[5]

On the other hand, the bourgeois elements that remained were characteristically materialistic in manifesting their utopian faith in the future. Insignificantly ugly little chapels gave place to pretentiously ugly pseudo-Gothic structures, to the everlasting memory of the local magnate who thus generously added his "mite" to the greater glory of God. Not one of them was ever endowed for its upkeep; and in a few years, with dwindling congregations and increasing costs, they have laid a burden of sentiment on succeeding generations that effectively smothered the churches' witness.

15

Nevertheless, the period up to the outbreak of World War I was one of unbounded optimism in the English Free Churches. They had freed themselves from the stigmas of second-class citizenship, and vindicated the "Free Church Idea." They were actively freeing themselves from the narrowness of their older theologies, and intellectually vying with Anglican scholarship in adapting theology to the new age. They shared with the rest of their countrymen unlimited belief in the material and spiritual progress of Britain, the British Empire,[6] the World—and themselves. All things seemed to unite in the principles they advocated, for Dr. Powicke's "free and open encounter whereby the truth can come to its own" was simply the intellectual counterpart of the free trade that had been so successful for them in the marketplace. They could look forward to a time of increasing influence and liberalization in politics, society, and religion.

Of course, there were a few Jeremiahs. W. B. Selbie uneasily remarked in 1908 that "the Free Churches, as they are now called, are suffering from their very prosperity. With the removal of serious disabilities, the advance in social status, and the triumph of their principles in many directions, has come a certain slackening in their hold on the great fundamentals of their ecclesiastical faith. They are even a little afraid of the old enthusiasms, and are in danger of drifting into mere opportunism."[7] But even in these sentences one discerns some smug satisfaction underneath, which leads us to question whether this was the voice of prophetic concern or of a Nonconformity that took its pleasures sadly.

That was the situation the English Free Churches enjoyed during the first decade or so of this century. (Remember that we are speaking about denominations that have transplanted themselves with great success into the history and life of America and dedicated

16

themselves to many of the ideals that Americans have regarded as sacred.) They were prosperous, influential, and confident that the future was theirs. If they were, as good liberals, critical of some features of Britain's national life and imperial policy, they nonetheless enjoyed its wealth and used its prestige. By 1914 they had gone far in freeing themselves from the biblicism of their older theologies, and many of their younger men were socially conscious enough to have freed themselves from the earlier economic orthodoxies.[8] They were progressive in almost every sense and only too ready to adapt their faith to the needs of the new age. "A modern theology," protested P. T. Forsyth in 1907, "is not simply theology *à la mode*."[9] Indeed it was precisely their all-out desire to achieve modernity and relevance that led Forsyth, who was certainly no biblical literalist, to take his stand against what he could only regard as an erosion of the Christian faith.

This is a situation, I suggest, that bears comparison with that of the American churches in the generation that followed World War II. The point of this historical comparison becomes clear if we go on to compare the Free Church expectations with the reality that developed. The mood of optimistic euphoria was dealt a mortal blow in the years 1914-18 and the *coup de grace* 1939-45. Within a period of roughly forty years these denominations lost approximately one-third of their membership,[10] but even more important was their loss of effective influence on public opinion and the life of the country. A. J. Cummings, a leading journalist of the Liberal daily *The News-Chronicle*, commented sadly in 1952 that the "Nonconformist conscience," which had controlled the thermometer of Liberal political policy, "is like a faint echo of its former glory," and he added wistfully, "The still small voice may survive; but we can hardly hear it now."[11] More recently Malcolm

Muggeridge observed, "Already most of the Nonconformist denominations are at their last gasp, and the Anglican Church is sustained only by the ostensible importance and actual revenue derived from its connection with the State."[12] We may question whether the institutions of Nonconformity can be quite so sweepingly dismissed, but there is certainly little comfort to be drawn from the statistics: the denominations have declined, are declining, and have a negligible effect on the cultural ethos and spiritual life of the country as a whole. From a practical point of view the devastating decline in actual membership has meant that the English churches have had to face a world of unprecedented demands and opportunities with rapidly dwindling resources. Year by year a greater proportion of their resources in wealth and personnel has had to be deployed in maintaining the very structures and institutions that were so optimistically created as centers for service and action a few decades ago.

* * *

The experience of the British Free Churches during the first half of this century should have been a warning to the American churches, for the parallels are too clear to be missed. But the warning has been entirely disregarded. Until very recently American churchmen were sympathetic but incredulous about what had happened in Britain, and fully confident that "it couldn't happen here" because "God is written into our Constitution," or because "we maintain the complete separation of church and state." This attitude was typical when I arrived in America in 1958.

What has happened since then? This confident, complacent attitude of the churches has been utterly exploded by the events of the 1960s. A new mood of skepticism has swept the country—skepticism about human goals and national policy as well as about religion (and the relationship between these is not accidental). The change of mood is certainly due in part to the cultural and scientific revolution that has seen the shrinking of the world with supersonic airliners and communications satellites, the flight of men to the moon, the arrival of the computerized micro-electronic society, and the transplanting of human organs. On the one hand it questions man's dependence on nature, God, or anything else, while on the other it presents us with problems, like pollution and population control, that we have not begun to answer, and which cannot be answered except in full community with the rest of the world's peoples. We are forced into the brotherhood of mankind with an inadequate ethical equipment, and we face questions that the old religious principles and the old ethics are unable to grasp.

Taking a broader view of history, it seems that the storms of popular skepticism arise wherever men are faced with a radically changed situation that the old faiths cannot explain or comprehend. A mood of skepticism is always associated with a time of revolution, because the accepted patterns of life are being shattered, and men begin to look around for new faiths — new myths — on which to base their world and their own place in it. It indicates that any society makes use of religion or pseudo-religion to support and explain its own structure and way of life. This was the position of the Free Churches in pre-World War I England, and the "revolution" was caused by the shock conventional thinking suffered in the death of a million British men in World War I, the failure of the League of Nations, and the menace of 1939-45. We should face the fact that if the churches in America were popular after 1945, the reasons were not to be sought in their "rightness" but in their service to the American way of life. That is not necessarily to condemn out of hand either the churches or the American way of life, but simply to recognize the reasons for popularity for what they are. It should cause the church to re-examine its gospel and ask some honest questions of itself about the relative value it sets on popular appeal and fidelity to the truth.

Conformism is a subtle tempter. It does not always support the *status quo*. Once the public mood begins to be skeptical of society and its institutions an opposite conformism enters into the picture. When the bandwagon of popular approval abruptly changes course, the church may find itself jettisoned as a supporter of the old "establishment" with a lot of other excess and outdated baggage or dismissed as an escape from reality. It then becomes fashionable to discard all that the new trend-setters ignore or ridicule, and to damn all those who do not have the "courage" to support the revolution.

Trying to catch the tailgate of the new trend may be equally dangerous for the church, for this too is simply a cultural fashion. This is the temptation that we face today, for we are rapidly being forced to recognize the grip of a social revolution that is turning conventional concepts and prejudices upside down. I suggest that the proper role of the church is neither blindly to react in a diehard support of the older establishments, which often granted popularity for quite the wrong reasons, nor is it to tag on blindly to the new bandwagon, but to take its prophetic call seriously, to take another look at its gospel, and to recognize in thought and action the prophetic word it should be declaring to all societies and cultures. Indeed, nothing argues more strongly the utter irrelevance of a church and the spuriousness of its message than to see it vainly trying to hitch a ride on each popular trend as it comes along.

Since 1960 a succession of events has accelerated the church's questioning about itself: the pointed sociological critique of the suburban churches and the recognition that the denominations had largely abandoned the inner city, the heavily publicized if short-lived "Death of God" theology and the debate initiated by Harvey Cox's *The Secular City*, the running sore of the war in Indochina and the resultant radical questioning of national policy, the realization that grinding poverty thrives in the midst of the affluent society, the civil rights movement and the recognition of the churches' own *de facto* segregation, turmoil in universities and colleges and growing alienation of youth, the Black Power movement and the Red Power movement, riots in the streets and violence on the reservation, the incredible assassinations of John Kennedy, Martin Luther King, Jr., and Robert Kennedy.

It is not our business to argue the rights and wrongs of these events. Some of them were tragic and cannot be recalled; some of them were concerned with justice and could not be avoided; some have been simply bizarre. But all have contributed to the present anxiety of the church in America, and in particular to anxiety about its own nature and purpose. I would maintain that it is the lack of unanimity on this issue that is responsible for the growing reluctance of church members to foot the bill for programs launched by their chosen leaders. It reflects a polarization within the church that is fundamentally a disagreement about the church's nature and function in society.

The decline is also shown by other indicators. The Special Report on Religion of the Gallup Public Opinion Index (1969) reveals that between 1958 and 1968 church attendance declined by six percentage points. Even more disquieting, among young adults attendance dropped by fourteen percentage points. Furthermore, an overwhelming number of those interviewed had no doubt that the church was declining in its influence upon the life of the country — over 67 percent felt this way in 1968 compared with only 14 percent ten years earlier.

The trend to secularism is not as far advanced in America as in most European countries, but the figures are solid enough to show that it *is* a trend and that it is in the same direction.

* * *

The approaching storm is real enough, and the reasons for the dramatic change in the church's situation are complex, but no serious Christian could think that the challenge of our time should be met simply by improved techniques or new gimmickry. Christians have to face the relation of their faith to the pressures of the present and the future — the tension between the legitimate demand for "relevance" and the equally legitimate demand that the church remain faithful to the gospel entrusted to it. This is an area of theological apologetic beyond our present scope. Furthermore, part of the challenge comes to its focus in the church itself, in the church's essential nature as the advocate and living exemplar of its own faith. No parts of the church's proclamation are more open to criticism, more undermined by the cultural revolution of our time, or more obviously a denial of what they were intended to exemplify than the forms that the traditional Protestant and Catholic doctrines of the church have assumed. However, even that is not our primary concern here.

We are concerned with the relation of the church to the fate of the race. The clear lesson of our time seems to be that the church is granted no immunity from the judgments of God in this world, because the church itself has been given to this world. But even less can the church expect to ensure its success or guarantee its security by an alliance with any secular culture or national society, no matter how affluent or powerful. God does not play favorites.

22

1 In 1871 the Liberals under Gladstone made an unsuccessful move to disestablish the Church of England. They were successful in respect to the Anglican Church in Ireland. The same year they obtained the removal of religious tests from the English universities. In 1912 Lloyd George introduced a bill for the disestablishment of the Church of Wales, which was bitterly contested; owing to the outbreak of World War I (1914-18) the bill was not finally passed until 1920. In the early years of the present century it looked as if the disestablishment of the Church of England would follow in a few years. That it did not is as much due to improved ecumenical relationships as to the decline of Nonconformity's political influence.

2 From the Restoration (1660), Nonconformists and Roman Catholics had been excluded from English universities (Oxford, Cambridge, Durham) and from other universities in Britain requiring subscription to Anglican tests (Trinity College, Dublin). These were removed in 1871. Earlier in the nineteenth century (1825) a group of Whigs, Nonconformists, and secularists had moved to establish University College, London, without religious tests, and this received royal charter in 1836.

3 It was not an accident that Karl Marx had concentrated his bitter attack of capitalism on industrial Britain, where the Industrial Revolution was further advanced than elsewhere. Nor were the dissenting antecedents of many of the industrialists accidental. They could provide classic examples of Max Weber's thesis in *The Protestant Ethic and the Spirit of Capitalism*. For the capitalist bias of Nonconformity see H. Lovell Cocks, *The Nonconformist Conscience* (London: Independent Press, 1943). Weber's "Protestant Ethic" only developed in its worst manifestations *after* the doctrine of the church became eroded in Protestantism. Up to that time the worst effects of the profit motive could be held in bounds by the effective

23

employment of church discipline—which, it should be noted, Calvinism added to the "preaching of the word" and the administration of the sacraments as an essential mark of the church. Cf. Robert S. Paul, "Weber and Calvinism: the Effects of a 'Calling,'" *Canadian Journal of Theology*, Vol. XI (1965), No. 1, pp. 25ff.

4 Dr. F. J. Powicke, as quoted by W. B. Selbie in *Mansfield College Essays*, presented to Principal A. M. Fairbairn on his seventieth birthday in 1908 (London: Hodder & Stoughton, 1909), p. 34.

5 *Jesus Rediscovered* (Garden City, N.Y.: Doubleday, 1969), pp. 33f., 37.

6 This should not necessarily be interpreted in a jingoistic way. Among Free Churchmen the concept of the British Empire pointed inevitably to self-government, local autonomy, and hence to the idea of a commonwealth of self-governing nations. There is an interesting example that deserves to be preserved. It was a sermon preached to young people in Oxton Road Congregational Church, Birkenhead, in 1896. In the course of his discourse the preacher used this illustration: "I may illustrate the point by a reference to national affairs. Each nation claims the right to manage itself, and so to decide its own destiny. But at the present England controls India. The inhabitants of a small island dominate nearly 300,000,000 of people. That, surely, is not an ideal condition of things. It may be granted that, at present, we are able to govern the country better than the Indians. But our aim must be so to develop their national life that, if not now, they shall ere long be able to govern their own country. The sooner they can do it, the more to our credit; and therefore every claim they put forth which, if granted, would conduce to this end, we dare not deny, since it is in line with their highest development." This sermon illustrates "Nonconformist conscience" in British politics in a more positive light than that in which it is usually presented. It is usually condemned for its restrictive

sabbatarianism and prohibitionism; few have given it credit for its support of political freedom. "Rights and Duties," by the Rev. Matthew Stanley (Birkenhead: E. W. Brimmell, 1896), p. 5.

7 *Mansfield College Essays*, pp. 34f.

8 A series of controversies in the late nineteenth century revolved around the issue of theological liberalism — the "Rivulet" controversy in Congregationalism, regarding the hymns of Thomas Toke Lynch; the heresy trial of McLeod Campbell in Scottish Presbyterianism; and the "Downgrade Controversy," which led the conservative preacher Charles Haddon Spurgeon to leave the Baptist Union. See John W. Grant, *Free Churchmanship in England, 1870-1940* (London: Independent Press, n.d.) and Willis B. Glover, *Evangelical Nonconformists and Higher Criticism in the 19th Century* (London: Independent Press, 1954).

9 *Positive Preaching and the Modern Mind* (London: Hodder & Stoughton, n.d. [1907]), p. 29.

10 The figures for the Congregationalists may be taken as representative. They reached their high point in 1915, when Congregationalists numbered 291,128. By 1930 they had declined to 276,540, but by 1959 they had reached 188,870. Cf. R. Tudur Jones, *Congregationalism in England 1662-1962* (London: Independent Press, 1962), pp. 387, 461f.

11 "The Struggle for the Soul of Man," *News-Chronicle*, April 3, 1952. There is a close parallel between the decline of Nonconformity and the decline of the parliamentary Liberal Party. The *News-Chronicle* itself, with a history dating back to the foundation of *The Daily News* in 1846 under the editorship of Charles Dickens, was bought out by the conservative *Daily Mail* in 1960.

12 Cf. *Jesus Rediscovered*, pp. 37, 41f.

Chapter 2

The Parable of the Storm

> *And now God enters the pulpit, and preaches in his own way by deeds. And his sermons are long and taxing, and they spoil the dinner. Clearly God's problem with the world is much more serious than we dreamed.*
>
> — P. T. Forsyth, *The Justification of God*

Let us return to the parable of the storm. Jeffrey K. Hadden has written of a "gathering storm within the churches," the turmoil surging up within the churches themselves due to the crises in belief, authority, and self-identity.[1] What he writes is real enough, and from the point of view of the church's own self-understanding and mission, it probably represents the most acute crisis for theology; but in comparison with that which confronts us in the whole human dilemma, it appears to be but a storm in a teacup. For all who are concerned about the problems threatening our survival know that the most obvious and immediate question is not how to save the church or any other institution, but how to save humanity, at the most elementary and existential level — how to prevent it from wiping the human species from this earth.

All other speculative questions are secondary, for if mankind succeeds in extirpating itself or becomes transmuted into something essentially less than human, subtle questions of ecclesiology will not matter very much. And this is the real possibility that is before us. As Gabriel Marcel has said, "I have a conviction that we are in a situation without precedent, which I would briefly define by saying that suicide has become possible on the scale of humanity itself. It is impossible to think of this situation and follow it to its logical conclusion without becoming aware that every one of us is almost at every moment faced by this fundamental choice, and he contributes by what he thinks, what he does and what he is, to increase or reduce the chances of this generalised suicide."[2] He is not alone in this concern.

Read the signs of the times. Whether we count ourselves as Christian, Buddhist, agnostic, Marxist, we are conscious that the immediate problem is with man, the final enemy is the death *in us*. Unless mankind is saved from itself, all intellectual speculation will be irrelevant. For it is the possibility of the eschaton that we face. Nothing appears more pointless in the present situation than the thought of theologians solemnly engaging in their trade and discussing ecclesiology while the world hovers on the brink of doom. If this final possibility is the one we face, our major concern should be with humanity here and now, our own humanity and the humanity of others, and our energies should be entirely devoted to saving that within the "here and now." Unless that salvation is achieved, there is no future for any of our institutions, however revered or sacred.

This is the basic and growing mood, and it explains many of the distinctive characteristics of the "Now Generation." The typical world-view of Western man is no longer governed by the image of the medieval castle with its banqueting hall above and its dungeons below,

27

but by that of the one-story ranch house (or at most a split-level), where we eat drink, work, make love, take our ease, indulge in religion (if we care to), suffer, and die — all on more or less the same level of existence. Virtually no effort is required to move from one activity to the other. No part of the traditional religious faith is received with more skepticism by moderns than that which affirmed life after death and a reciprocal system of divine reward and punishment. Although belief in heaven and hell is still more prevalent in the United States than in Europe (85% of the people questioned in a 1969 survey said they still believed in heaven; 65% said they believed in hell), the change in Europe over the past twenty years has been striking. As the authors of the survey comment, "a dramatic change has taken place in many European countries," and particularly "in terms of belief in life after death."[3] It is important to understand these signs of the times, for in this case the theological weather to be expected in America comes from the east.

This change in belief about life after death in Western man is the great psychological difference between all the previous ages of faith and the people of the mid-twentieth century. In the first decade of this century P. T. Forsyth pointed out that Protestant ministers could no longer assume that people read their Bibles, and he said that preachers would therefore have to "adjust our preaching to the people's disuse of the Bible."[4] In a similar way, in proclaiming the note of judgment, the church today has to recognize that for a large number of people the old pictorial and punitive categories of heaven and hell make little sense, and for an increasing number of our contemporaries the prospect of anything beyond this existence on earth is meaningless.

Once this climate of opinion becomes general, the whole world-view in Western society will have been adically changed, if not turned upside down. The principle voiced by the "rich fool" of the New Testament, "Eat, drink and be merry, for tomorrow we die," will no longer be the height of folly but a proposition deserving careful consideration and will be regarded by most as a statement of sober realism. A growing number of people believe that all we can experience has to be experienced here and now. This life is it. As the television commercial says, you have to grab all the gusto you can, because you only go around once.

The issue of peace and war simply gives the demand for life a greater urgency. Our contemporaries want peace now because it is the guarantee of everything else that is desirable in life; but beyond this they demand social, political, and economic justice *now*, freedom to be oneself without limitation or inhibition *now*, complete financial and medical security *now*. And insofar as religion has been used by unscrupulous politicians and charlatans to postpone the just demands of oppressed peoples for a better life now, it has been used as the opium of the people. To those convinced of a one-story universe, however, the imperative needs of this life are the things that really matter, and anything that postpones them to an indefinite future on earth or beyond or makes their realization conditional on conformity and good behavior is pernicious and intolerable. It is the insistent claim of Esau against Jacob (Gen. 25: 29-34), in which birthrights have to give place to the appetites of here and now.

Of course there have always been those who have had this view of life and destiny from Omar Khayyam onwards. Andrew Marvell gave expression to it in the seventeenth century in the lines to his coy mistress:

> *Had we but world enough, and time,*
> *This coyness, Lady, were no crime. . . .*
> *But at my back I always hear*

> *Time's winged chariot hurrying near;*
> *And yonder all before us lie*
> *Deserts of vast eternity.*

The only difference now is that this attitude, once the life-style of a small minority, is well on the way to becoming that of the majority; and it already represents the philosophy accepted by many of the sophisticated and most admired sections of the public. Furthermore, despite what is confessed in church and despite the centrality of the resurrection in the New Testament, this philosophy is tacitly accepted by many churchgoers and for all practical purposes governs the way they live their lives and plan their careers. The urgency has moved from concern with an eschatological but hypothetical future fate to concern with an existential but wholly real fate that confronts us in this life.

This is where the church faces the imperative question set by our age. If this earthly life is all and if our race is threatened by alternative dooms that are equally absolute, why should men bother with the church — or, indeed, with any other than the immediate question of the survival of the race and the proximate question of wringing from the moment as much happiness as possible? Obviously if one is to justify the expenditure of the time spent in reading or writing this book rather than in demonstrating at the Pentagon or devising a quicker means of committing suicide, a large "But . . ." must be introduced.

* * *

Before that can be introduced, however, there must be an explanation at the personal level. It is not suggested that the pages that follow can take the place of a full Christian eschatology. They are written from a Christian point of view by one who is still convinced that I Corinthians 15 stands at the center of the New

Testament proclamation, not because it reflects man's wistful desire to avoid the ultimacy of death, but because it confirms something essential about the nature of the God who spoke his word in Jesus Christ.[5] Moreover, I also happen to believe that when the apostle Paul said he would eventually know himself with the kind of completeness with which he was even then known by God (I Cor. 13:12f.), he was recognizing that we all have to come face to face with the judgment of God's love in Christ. To some that will sound too conservative; to others it will be much too liberal — though for me personally those terms have become totally irrelevant. The point I wish to stress is that the ensuing pages are offered not as an alternative eschatology, but as a starting-place for the twentieth-century proclamation.

Traditional Christianity had a cosmic view with three distinct levels: heaven, with its "cloud of witnesses" (Heb. 12:1) and church triumphant; the earth, where we strive and prove ourselves within the church militant; and hell, where those who failed the test pay the price of their sins. Heaven and hell were seen as a little cooler or a little hotter, more material or more spiritualized, according to the theological preferences of the preacher, but that was the general pattern.

But — and this is the "but" on which the twentieth-century issue hinges — what happens if the one-story universe is taken at its face value?[6] What happens if we take modern man's evaluation of human destiny as the working basis for the Christian proclamation, not because that is all there is to the Christian's faith, but because it is the only stance that our contemporaries can understand? Judgment has certainly not disappeared. Surely there is significance in the fact that judgment on our race now invades our time, that man has not escaped an ultimate judgment simply by eliminating the eschatological finality of it from his consciousness? Surely whether we believe in heaven or hell or not, whether or not we are able to stomach the idea of a last judgment in terms of medieval saccharinity or gruesomeness, mankind *is* being judged here and now. The wrath of God is real. God has brought the threat of the hell we create for ourselves and the prospect of the heaven into which we could be called right into our present time for the convenience of those who insist on living in a one-story universe. He has brought it home to us by bringing it to the place where we cannot avoid the issue any longer, right on our affluent, twentieth-century doorstep.

If we solve the problems of our human condition, which, even if they are not understood as religious, may certainly be seen to be ethical, a future of unimagined beauty and happiness seems to be waiting for the human race. If we do not solve them, or if we simply ignore problems caused by our own greed and callousness, the result will be a hell of unimagined horror and a damnation for our race that is final and complete. Whether or not the bizarre imagery of the medieval artists is credible to twentieth-century man, this possibility is right here — a hell in which we will continue with increasing brutality and efficiency to butcher each other in quiet ongoing massacres along the overcrowded borders (do you remember those continuous frontier wars in *1984*?) as we fight for the last free pockets of land, water, and air, or in which we all evaporate in nuclear holocaust. It may be a hell in which we suffocate in the Stygian stench of our own garbage and excrement, or starve through the rapacity that has eroded nature into a desert; or a hell in which through genetic powers a government of élite scientists programs the rest of us into contented servitude. Ever since World War II Western man has shuddered before the twin horrors of a completely totalitarian society and the prospect of nuclear extinction.

The fears may have been groundless, but they have been nonetheless real.

Perhaps our greatest danger is to dismiss these nightmares as science fiction or preacher's rhetoric. They are not. They represent the real possibilities of our human condition. Hell—the composite of all the hells described above — has been brought into our time and can overtake us within the next few decades unless we solve the root problems, which are essentially ethical. This has little to do with whether one is politically and religiously "radical" or "conservative"; read the Great Assize (Matt. 25:31-45) and interpret it if you will in terms of a judgment in this world here and now. Read it and apply it to yourself whether your preferred excuses are radical or conservative. Within the context of this life that we claim as our own we are being forced to see that we bear responsibility for the judgment being made by history on our race, and this apart from all other considerations ought to bring back the note of urgency to our proclamation of the gospel. Even for those whose view of human destiny is limited to the dimension of present experience, the day of decision cannot be postponed. God is not mocked. God *cannot* be mocked indefinitely and with impunity, because righteousness cannot be mocked with impunity without finally destroying the unrighteous society that does the mocking.

* * *

We may approach the same issue in a slightly different way. The twentieth-century temperament finds almost insuperable aesthetic and ethical barriers to believing in the old hell-fire, blood-and-thunder God whom our forefathers seem to have had no difficulty in accepting. The problem has been expressed very clearly in an English detective novel, in which the police officer

33

in charge of investigating the seditious actions of a strange apocalyptic sect pondered on the preacher's fulminations and his vivid descriptions of souls burning in hell. The policeman "wondered mildly if Zebedee had ever seen a human being in flames," as he had during his war service, and he could not help going on to speculate about the psychological make-up of people who imagine the destiny of the cosmos is in the hands of such a God.[7] Of course. When this view of God is turned into essential dogma we are brought into violent and irreconcilable conflict with the nature revealed to us in Jesus Christ.

On the other hand, we easily fall into the opposite error of thinking that we can define God in our own terms. This is to make him just as much an idol. God is not so circumscribed; his nature is not to be limited to our casual, twentieth-century complaisance and easy tolerance. By insisting that God's nature is governed by the moral standards that we recognize as the highest, we are trying to set up a god in our own image. Certainly that which we recognize as God must include the highest that we know, but his highest is not to be confined to our highest, nor can his highest be limited to what we know. As Forsyth said of our Lord, "Christ is ours not because He represents our best but because he redeems our worst."[8] If there is any gospel, there is always that which comes from the outside, which cannot be limited to our human categories. The term "God" not only by definition but also by revelation and experience cannot be exhaustively defined. If we try to set its boundaries, to specify its content and precisely describe the character and qualities of that which we are defining, our definition has already failed because we can never fully express what men confess when they worship "God." Any definition can only approximate the truth that has been revealed, and for twentieth-century man there is in the concept "God" an element of ruthless simplicity that he finds difficult to assimilate.

Without reverting to metaphysics or chiding the modern generation in the name of a revelation it is not prepared to recognize, we would perhaps do better to remind it once again of its own human situation, which it cannot deny and dare not ignore. There appears to be a disconcerting simplicity in nature, which religious liberals refuse to incorporate into their theology, perhaps because it is an embarrassment to their view of providence, and which religious conservatives reject because it is an embarrassment to their dogmatic view of creation. This is the principle of the survival of the fittest, the simple law in nature that species that do not measure up to the conditions and the needs are destroyed by their own defects.

A twentieth-century skeptic has little difficulty in accepting this principle, for it ties him to no theology, seems to be scientifically verifiable, and can be regarded as impersonal and mechanistic in its operation. But we are up against one of the great paradoxes of creation, because at heart the principle is entirely redemptive. This process of cosmic pragmatism seems to have operated not because of any vindictiveness on the part of "Nature," but in order to ensure the health and fitness of the whole creation and to advance the purpose of that creation in the most effective way. It is surgery, but it is redemptive surgery, and in some way we have to recognize that this ordered ruthless simplicity also belongs to God and his purpose in history.

At a much higher level, Peter Berger recognized the ruthlessness of this simplicity at the heart of things in *The Precarious Vision*. He protests against the punitive violence through which nations and societies establish their control over people, and points out that the justification for such punitive violence is provided in our written records: we turn to the documents and the books to provide historical precedents, to argue our case, or to present our credentials, whether it is in justification of war or capital punishment. "The judge can point to the statute books, the governor to the constitution of the state, the warden to the prison regulations, and so forth. Any literate man can easily verify the authenticity of the claims. It is most unfortunate that God is illiterate. He has read neither statute books nor the constitution of the state, nor the prison regulations. . . . God would not be God if he recognized these delusions as the truth."[9] God in fact judges men as human beings who bear responsibility to other human beings, and not in terms of their elaborate justifications or excuses. Berger may no longer hold precisely these same views,[10] but I am sure he was theologically correct to insist on this essential simplicity in the nature of God; and as he showed, such simplicity, even as it is offered in love, can be utterly ruthless.

The Old Testament does often present us with the figure of a Bronze Age God. Within its pages are attributed to him cruelties that disgust the finer susceptibilities of the modern, who oddly enough has been able to stomach the two bloodiest world wars in history, the attempted genocide of the Jews, and now makes a habit of bringing the latest vicious conflicts, whether in Southeast Asia, the Indian subcontinent, or the Middle East, into his living room by means of television. If our only true theology is anthropology, as I heard a brash young theological dean remark a few years ago, we cannot even exclaim "God help us!" Yet twentieth-century man is right to be disgusted with the literal interpretation of the Old Testament God and to protest against the anthropomorphism that makes savagery and vindictiveness part of God's essential nature.

On the other hand, what the biblical record points to,

often with a realism for which we are totally unprepared, is that there is a ruthless simplicity at the center of history that is implacably set against sin and evil and brings down civilizations through their own inner corruption. It is a testimony against social sin not only because it is wholly incompatible with God's nature, but also because it is wholly destructive of man's nature. Just as there is a redemptive ruthlessness in nature that prevents corrupt or defective species from flourishing indefinitely lest they should corrupt everything, so there is the same process at work in societies and civilizations. Perhaps this is the ultimate mystery of mercy in providence with which we have to come to terms. Certainly we reject the literalism that revels in the more gory characteristics of Yahweh and attempts to give them the same authority as a revelation of God's nature as the Sermon on the Mount or the passion of our Lord, but that does not mean that the truth to which these incidents point should be rejected out of hand. I suggest that these early portrayals of the God of history are pointing to the basic laws that govern the historical process, of cause and effect, of selection and discard, of sin and retribution, through which alone the creation with its infinite possibilities for progress will be preserved. And if our race turns its back on those laws, it must fall under their judgment.

* * *

There is a persistent apocalypticism in the Bible that cannot be ignored. It reveals a redemptive necessity within the human condition, without which the human race cannot find its own salvation, materially or spiritually. There is no settlement in the promised land without slavery in Egypt, trauma at the Red Sea, and years wandering in the wilderness. There is no restoration of the nation and the temple without the experience of defeat and exile. There is no resurrection apart from

37

the crucifixion. And there is no advent of the kingdom in power without the prospect of final judgment. This, too, belongs to the revelation of God's will and nature, and perhaps we are being reminded of it. As Forsyth remarked at the beginning of this century, "the attractive piety of incipient culture, with its atmosphere of young bustle, good form, genial love, kindly conference, and popular publications, is without the great note of New Testament realism and imagination; and is therefore at an utter loss when the world is shocked and forced upon the question of a theodicy."[11] Forsyth saw the failure of twentieth-century religion more clearly than we do.

Yet the judgment on men and nations that the Bible recognizes is written into history not because God is vindictive — the crucified Christ is the judge in the Apocalypse — but because he is a God of redemptive love who cannot permit man's sin to destroy the creation. C. S. Lewis saw the point when he reflected on the possibility of men's going as missionaries to the planets in distant galaxies and asked whether "the vast astronomical distances may not be God's quarantine precautions. They prevent the infection of a fallen species from spreading."[12]

The apocalyptic passages in the Bible, used literally, have been a devastating weapon in the hands of simple revolutionaries who burn with an intolerable sense of injustice. Like the followers of Thomas Müntzer or the crazed Anabaptists of Münster at the time of the Reformation, their literalism can push them to cruelties and excesses that must be deplored, but we cannot deplore their outrage at injustice or their conviction that God will not tolerate evil forever. They may not present an adequate picture of the God who meets us in the Bible, but they certainly have some insight into that which is at work in our own nature and history.

38

Those same apocalyptic passages (e.g. II Tim. 3:1-5; I Thess. 5:1-8; Rev. 22:9-15) denounce the *social* sins, the sins of self-indulgence, greed, and hedonism that have been characteristic of civilizations in decline all through history. We can agree that self-righteous prophets of all ages have often been tempted to wallow in the threat of destruction and vengeance and to gloat over the fate of the wicked; and we may agree, too, that these sins of spiritual pride are ultimately nastier and as destructive to them personally as the very sins they denounce. But the evils that the Bible denounces in these passages are the social evils, the blatant evils that destroy nations and cultures rather than the secret sins that destroy the individual; and it is with the evils of society that we are concerned here and now, for we are concerned with the survival of the race.

* * *

Where does this get us? It gets us to the point where we should again begin to take seriously the reality of judgment in history, and to recognize that we do not get rid of it or of the moral imperatives involved in it simply by discarding the outdated imagery in which it was handed to us. Heaven and hell are real options, and we are now brought inescapably face to face with the issue in this present time. This should bring back the note of urgency into our proclamation not only by reminding our fellow man of the lateness of the hour, but also by reminding us all that the decisions we are now making are irrevocable. It also shows the integral relationship between the church and the world, by emphasizing the solidarity of the race, the unity of decision, suffering, and possible glory into which we are all caught, and the significance of the cosmic Christ that we find in Paul and Irenaeus.

The Christian faith is not exhausted by the experience

of twentieth-century man, but if that is where we have to start in order to claim his attention, let us begin there and honestly face its implications. Forsyth advised the divinity students at Yale in 1907 to "learn not to say so much to your people of a day of Judgment sure though far. The farness destroys the sureness. Ethicize the reality of judgment. Moralize the eschatology. Couple it up to the hour. Drop, if need be, the drapery of the remote assize. The judge is at the door. Everything comes home. It comes home in calamity if you do not take it home in repentance."[13] Although Forsyth did not have *1984* and its attendant threats in prospect, the issue could not have been expressed more aptly.

The gospel proclaims that there is an uncivilized, searing mercy at the center of history, which has established the strict laws of cause and effect in order to protect this erring human race. For those prepared to listen, it also declares that this same mercy has been prepared to step down, to identify with the human in its failure, and to take the effects upon itself. This is the good news. But at the level of secular institutions where faith and penitence do not often operate, this same redemptive ruthlessness allows nations and civilizations to destroy themselves, so that the rottenness which has corrupted them from within does not spread to the whole creation. This is why the meaning of apocalyptic in the Bible and the warning of its fanatic revolutionary exponents should be heeded. We must read the signs of our times in all their complex simplicity.

1 *The Gathering Storm in the Churches* (New York: Doubleday, 1969).

2 From *Les hommes contre l'humain*, as quoted by J. M. Perrin in *Forward the Layman (L'Heure des Laïcs)* (Westminster, Md., 1956), p. 25.

3 In Greece, which is the country with the next highest figures after the United States, 65% of those interviewed confessed belief in heaven and 62% belief in hell. Over the whole of Western Europe the average is 50% belief in heaven and 30% belief in hell. *Gallup Opinion Poll: Special Report on Religion*, February 1969, pp. 14, 16-17.

4 *Positive Preaching and the Modern Mind*, p. 36.

5 Paul put the issue very frankly for Christians when he declared, "If it is for this life only that Christ has given us hope, we of all men are most to be pitied" (I Cor. 15:19, NEB).

6 I acknowledge my debt in this section to an old friend, Rev. Basil Hudson Sims, who provided in conversation the anvil on which these ideas were hammered out. He should be absolved from any further responsibility for the views presented here.

7 Conrad Voss Bark, *The Second Red Dragon* (London: Victor Gollancz, 1968), p. 33.

8 *Positive Preaching and the Modern Mind*, p. 123.

9 *The Precarious Vision* (Garden City, New York: Doubleday, 1961), p. 193.

10 *The Sacred Canopy* (Garden City, New York: Doubleday, 1967), pp. 179ff., Appendix II.

11 *The Justification of God*, p. 5.

12 *The World's Last Night* (New York: Harcourt, Brace, 1952), p. 91.

13 *Positive Preaching and the Modern Mind*, p. 153.

Chapter 3

The Revolution to End All Revolutions

> Jesus Christ his work in the last days is to destroy this mystery of iniquity; and because it is so inter- woven and entwisted in the interests of states, cer- tainly in the overthrow of the mystery of iniquity by Jesus Christ, there must be great alteration of states. Now the word doth hold out in the Revelation, that in this work of Jesus Christ he shall have a company of Saints to follow him, such as are chosen and called faithful. Now it is a scruple among the Saints how far they should use the sword; yet God hath made use of them in that work.
> — Lt. Col. William Goffe, at the Putney Debates in 1647

> It is impossible to preach with reality to an age like this and ignore the social crisis and demand. We must face the questions put to the Gospel by a time which is passing from one social epoch to another.
> — P. T. Forsyth,
> Positive Preaching and the Modern Mind

We live in an age of revolution. True, the word "revo- lution" is open to several slightly different meanings, and insofar as we are all involved in massive social, economic, and cultural changes that seek a more just ordering of society, there would probably be general agreement that we live in an age of revolution, and considerable agreement that if a more just society is the objective, Christians must give their support.

But in some contexts, revolution implies as much about the means to be used as the ends to be achieved. It implies violence as the ultimate answer to the political dilemma, readiness to use any means of coercion to achieve the goal, willingness to commit murder, arson, blackmail, or any other effective crime in the book to gain the ultimate "good." It was the excuse given by Thomas Müntzer for the excesses of the Peasants' Revolt, by Robespierre for the Reign of Terror, and by Lenin for the massacres of the Russian Revolution.

In an age when revolution holds that possibility within it, the church faces a genuine dilemma, for not only is it faced with the tension between the demand for justice and the means employed to achieve it, but also the church's own history has been ambiguous. Hannah Arendt has suggested that Machiavelli may be "the spiritual father of revolution" in the sense we have come to know it, and pointed out that it is a comparatively recent phenomenon in human history.[1] We might go on to suggest that Machiavelli's studied use of violence for political purposes might never have taken a revolutionary form in the modern sense had not the Reformation broken the ancient alliance between church and state and democratized the issue by making every man responsible before God. In the context of the sixteenth- and seventeenth-century despotisms this insight very soon gained a political dimension, and it was no less a man than Oliver Cromwell who thought his son should be prepared for public service, "for which a man is born."[2] Revolution in the modern sense is a phenomenon of "the Protestant Era."

The relationship of revolution to Protestantism is, indeed, even closer, for in the past it has been clear that when Christians have become political revolutionaries as a sincere commitment arising from their understanding of the faith, they have done so on the basis of biblical literalism, and particularly literalism applied to the apocalyptic passages. There was a fever of expectation that the end was at hand at the time of the Peasants' Revolt in 1525, again during the incidents at Münster in 1534-36, and during the English Great Rebellion, whose Fifth Monarchists expected to enthrone King Jesus. It seems that almost invariably when Christians have turned to revolution as a political program, the literal expectation of the end as described in the Apocalypse provides the obvious justification for that clear-cut categorization of absolute good (us) and absolute evil (them) which is a moral necessity for revolutionaries in general and "Christian revolutionaries" in particular.

But there is the other side of the dilemma, for it is clear that even when rigorous literalism is applied to the interpretation of the New Testament, the issue is not as explicit as the apocalyptic revolutionaries would have us believe. Even if one thinks he has enlisted in the army of the militant Christ in Revelation and is ready to use the sword in his cause, what is to be made of our Lord's condemnation of Peter's sword play in the Garden of Gethsemane and his warning that "all who take the sword will perish by the sword"? What is one to make of the cross itself? Colonel Goffe was right, there is "a scruple among the Saints."

A more sensitive approach to Scripture cannot help noticing the special place that Jesus gave to the peacemakers and will recognize that the ministry of reconciliation became the particular responsibility of his followers. It will have to question whether in any Christian sense the end can ever justify the means, for violent methods obviously contrary to the spirit of the Jesus of the Gospels tend to pervert both the actors and their chosen objectives in the accomplishment. And there is the practical lesson of church history. Although many simple believers, outraged by the injustice of their time, have gone into battle expecting Armageddon to justify their bloodshed and to usher in the millennium, up to now they have been wrong. The time was not yet.

What, then, are we to say of our own part in these revolutionary times? In one sense, as we have seen, we face the realities of the eschaton in a much more existential way than Müntzer's misguided peasants or the fanatic Fifth Monarchists could have ever known. For many Christians in different parts of the world, the issue remains a genuine dilemma, which was illustrated by a responsible ecumenical churchman when he described the radically different attitudes taken by two black church leaders to their own political responsibility in this century. The first was the program of nonviolence begun by Martin Luther King; the other that of "a leader of one of the African liberation governments who is actively seeking by terrorism and violence to overthrow the colonial regime which still holds his people in Africa in bondage."[3] Both these men were professed Christians, and they personify the genuine dilemma that the churches have failed to solve.

Furthermore, it is clear that during the last half of the 1960s King's policy of nonviolence lost ground among his own people. Apart from the disillusionment caused by events, in a one-story universe it did not appear urgent enough. It did not guarantee results fast enough, and political cynicism led many to question just how far any established power structure will go unless it is forced. The new leaders want radical change; they want it now; and they believe that to achieve it one must be prepared for civil war. So a black American minister

45

declared in 1969 to the World Council of Churches Conference on Racial Justice in London, "When a society does not permit restructuring power that produces justice through economics and political maneuvers, then the church *ought not to shy away from aiding and abetting* the development of the only power available— which is *the power of violence.*"[4] There was a cartoon in the late 1960s showing a clergyman opening a package of guns and grenades, with the caption "Oh goody! The new social service material has just arrived." Despite the exaggeration we recognize that this cartoon reflected a new revolutionary mood among politically radical churchmen — a revolutionary mood based, it is true, no longer on the old biblical literalism of earlier periods, but perhaps no less apocalyptic in its ultimate appeal. Somehow violent revolution seems to be so much more respectable when the participants can convince themselves that they are engaging in a revolution to end all revolutions.

The dilemma cannot be "solved," for a Christian caught up in the kind of events that embroiled France in 1789 or Russia in 1917 is alone with his conscience. There are parts of this globe where the arguments of revolt by force may still offer the only hope of social or political reform, just as there are some relatively primitive societies in which rebellion very much on the traditional lines of 1789 or 1917 may still be possible.[5] If the reasons that Christians gave for violent revolution had any theological validity — and in view of our later knowledge, we must remind ourselves that that is an arguable question — then they would have validity in these places. But we are in a totally new situation. Because of the close relationship between expectation of the end and revolutionary involvement in the past, we must notice that there are unique aspects of the eschaton, which radically change the situation.

The new and decisive feature in our situation is that we have been brought to our present crisis in human affairs through the incredible development of technology, and in particular by the fact that we live in societies that are increasingly *controlled* by technology. The advent of the so-called technocracy raises the question, not whether revolution is desirable, nor even whether it is justifiable, but how far it is possible.

* * *

J. C. Hoekendijk hints at this in a passage where he discerns the shape and characteristic marks of the new humanity that is emerging. The "Fourth Man" of our immediate future is already beginning to take the place of the "Third Man," who was the secularized and proletarian product of classical-Christian culture. This emerging type of man, Hoekendijk says, cannot be given a name, although he might be known by number or cipher, and he can best be described as a "rebelling conformist." Hoekendijk draws an important distinction between rebellion and revolution. "Rebellion is the opposite of revolution. Revolution presupposes a historical plasticity: the belief that things can be different and the hope that we can bring that other day near. This faith and this hope the 'fourth' man has mainly lost. Wherever one looks one notices an *impotence to revolt*."[6]

It is not our purpose to argue about the details of this Orwellian nightmare, but only to note this characteristic "impotence to revolt" and to observe that it is technology which has made the completely regimented society possible. It is the élitist control of technology that is putting revolution out of range, whether that control is exercised by big business, by big government, or by a small in-group of the scientific community.

So the basic criticism of the kind of radical thinking that was noted earlier (apart from its tendency to sentimentalize "violence," as religious warmongers all through the ages have done) is its naive assumption that bloody revolution *can* still achieve liberal goals. I suggest that in the modern, scientifically efficient state, the time is rapidly passing, if it has not already passed, when revolution would be possible in the sense in which it has been known since the sixteenth century. In the United States, the Soviet Union, and Western Europe, revolution in the nineteenth-century sense may be as passé, from a practical point of view, as the colonial politics of that period: in the technocracies that have developed it is rapidly becoming, if it has not already become, obsolete. Indeed, it may be a subconscious realization that the sands of time are running out on this kind of political protest that is partially responsible for the frenetic attempt to get things moving on all fronts without delay.

Consider these facts about the emerging world we live in.

— Scientifically sophisticated nations have the technical knowledge and equipment necessary to exterminate or to reduce to impotence any internal dissent. What they normally lack is the ruthlessness to do this and the public opinion that would support such a policy, because in modern societies there is usually a considerable block of moderate opinion that the government (particularly in a democracy) prefers not to antagonize. Only a relatively extremist state disregards this opinion. Modern governments do not lack the means to impose uniformity, they lack only the climate of public opinion that would tolerate it.

— But as soon as the fighting starts in earnest, moderate opinion is the first casualty. It is under attack from both sides, because it is to the interests of the extremists of both wings to force people to take sides in *their* cause and upon *their* terms, or become a neatly defined "enemy." This explains why it was liberal schools like Cornell, Swarthmore, Harvard, and Brandeis that were first disrupted. The same attempt to enforce polarization was illustrated in the nonnegotiable demands made to predominantly liberal churches. Extremist opinion, whether of the right or the left, wishes to reduce the situation to clear-cut alternatives, and to push its advantages to the limit at the points of least resistance. In any kind of a crusade there is no place for neutrals, and once the situation has become polarized it is to the interest of both extreme parties to press this as far as it will go: "We are good, they are evil: we are of God, but they are of the devil." On with the crusade! On with the Inquisition!

— From the point of view of the extremist the purpose is well served if a "confrontation" produces some atrocities and a few martyrs. This has obvious publicity value and usually further widens the gap between the parties and helps to create a public opinion that will be sympathetic to the demand for "just retribution." Once the position has become completely polarized, a situation is created in which even the question of martyrdom becomes suspect if not meaningless, for the victorious party, whether "establishment" or "revolutionary," is left in complete political control. If revolution were to take place in a modern technocracy, it would leave the successful party totalitarian in temper and in complete possession of the technical means to eliminate all dissent.

— Tertullian was able to boast that the blood of the martyrs was the seed of the church, but martyrdom can only stimulate the response of faith when what is done is done openly, when men can know the facts and freely judge them. Tertullian's boast was true of the early church because the Roman Empire misjudged the effect of public martyrdoms on the population and exerted no control over how the facts were interpreted by the public.

Martyrdom today can be a valuable weapon in the hands of the reformers as long as the inquisitorial methods of reaction and the bravery of the martyrs can be given full publicity. But what happens when this possibility no longer exists, when publicity is used to broadcast the abject recantations of those who have been tortured and brainwashed *in camera*, or when the brave are spirited away to die in secret? What will such ambiguous and anonymous martyrdom mean to a generation that expects nothing beyond this life? Six million Jews were martyred in the space of a few years, literally under the noses of the German public, without producing any popular outcry. I do not think all German people were that callous; they were simply not allowed to know what was happening. The modern state can do that.

Even if the existing establishment is overthrown, a revolutionary society based on violence produces or becomes only an uglier and more cruel version of established authority. This could be illustrated from the course of campus violence at the end of the 1960s. John Lennon, who can hardly be accused of being unsympathetic to the student cause, recognized this in a 1969 interview: "The students are being conned! It's like the school bully: he aggravates you and aggravates you until you hit him. . . . The only thing they can't control is the mind, and we have to fight for sanity and peace on that level. *But the students have gotten conned into thinking you can change it with violence* and they can't, you know, they can only make it uglier and worse."[7]

But even if the escalation of violence does not have this result, it affects the participants of all persuasions. As Herbert Bau has commented: "In the revolutionary process they [students] have learned to lie, blackmail, and brutalize themselves in the provocation of the brutality they wanted to prove. No matter that they proved

50

it. The veil falls, the beast is exposed, and one sees his double. It happens even to people under thirty. *The wrench thrown into the machine to curb an insane momentum has released a brainless violence no better than brainless authority.*"[8]

That is the human dilemma. The unique and horrifying element in the situation today is the technical knowledge we now have of how men can be subjugated and the exquisite scientific means available for reducing them to impotence. All that is lacking is the mood of public opinion that would legitimate its use. Hitler and Stalin showed us the possibilities, and there are plenty of "school bullies" in our own society who would love the excuse to experiment.

*   *   *

Revolution was a relatively viable method of political action through the "Protestant Era," the age just prior to our own; and it was possible for three basic reasons.

In the first place, despite the horrors of the wars of religion (which represented revolution and counter-revolution), the opposing sides throughout these centuries recognized some common ethical standards and principles. There was a residue of "Christian values" or even national prejudices in favor of "fair play" that often prevented the antagonists from pushing a war to extermination. For example, despite all the bloodshed during the birthpangs of Bangladesh, a curious residue of the British Raj was noticeable in the "old-school-tie" attitude of the opposing generals in the Indo-Pakistani conflict of 1971.[9] The restraining influences were obviously more apparent in some cases than others — in the English Great Rebellion and the American Revolution than at the height of the religious wars or during the French and Russian Revolutions—but they often prevented both sides from pursuing the enemy to complete extinction.

Second, there were, through the end of the Protestant era, relatively large unoccupied parts of the globe, such as America, which provided a refuge for dissidents or *émigrés*. This too prevented thoroughgoing ideological extermination. Those who lost the ideological struggle in Europe could always escape to America where their ideas would live again. Today this kind of escape is less and less feasible: where is the "America" of the twentieth century?

Finally, the power to exterminate and control ideas efficiently was limited. No one had the technical knowledge capable of genocide or of maintaining surveillance and enforcing control over the individual to the extent possible today. Even through the wars of religion complete subjugation was rarely possible. The Treaty of Westphalia in 1648 recognized this by simply reinforcing the interim settlement of Augsburg (1555)—a localized, *de facto* acceptance by each side of the other's existence —and making this the permanent settlement for religion in Europe. Catholics and Protestants were forced to recognize that they did not have the power to destroy one another completely.

On the other hand, even during these earlier centuries, whenever the state had sufficient means to suppress the opposition, whenever it could prevent flight abroad, and whenever it was prepared to act with sufficient ruthlessness, dissent was totally eradicated. Sixteenth-century Spain's treatment of Protestants and Moriscoes is a clear example. If others did not succeed as completely as Philip II, it was not because they lacked the will, but because they lacked the means to make their policy effective.[10]

Furthermore, we should notice that true revolutions develop a tendency to become dictatorships, with a frank reliance on military or police power.[11] If these dictator-ships of the past could not be called "totalitarian" in the twentieth-century meaning of that word, it was only because the governing powers did not have the technical means by which to maintain control of their populations.[12]

Today this is no longer true. A revolution in a modern, technically efficient state would result in virtual dictator-ship, whether power was won finally by a revolutionary government or retained by the existing establishment. Science places a complete range of weapons in the hands of centralized authority. Virtually instantaneous communications and electronic means of surveillance make it practically impossible for a revolutionary move-ment to ferment for long undetected. "Truth drugs" and the refinements of brainwashing make the older methods of torture obsolete. Perhaps the most disquiet-ing development in recent years is the rate at which genetic control is becoming a possibility. It obviously holds enormous possibilities for good or evil, but the direction in which the new powers are used will inevi-tably be determined by whoever has the authority to control their use.[13] And, in the last resort, genocide is possible on an unprecedented scale. The horrors de-scribed in *1984* are possible. If we find that unthinkable it is not because the controls are scientifically impos-sible but because in our present frame of mind we cannot stomach it. Our situation is unique because of the actual possibility of scientific control over almost every phase of human life and destiny. Dissent *can* be utterly crushed. All that is wanting is the public opinion that would legitimate such action and allow the control-ling powers to be free to act. And the bloodiness of the revolution itself would soon provide this climate of opinion.

If this is a correct estimate of our situation, we must

append to any ethical questions we have about revolution here and now a little more skepticism on purely pragmatic grounds. In the developing situation it will be fatal if those who wish to see radical reform in society allow even their most passionately held political preferences to intoxicate their intelligence. We still enjoy a relative freedom to express dissent from the government, and this must be safeguarded at all costs.

* * *

All this obviously has serious political implications,[14] but it seems to be a long way from any direct relationship with the church.

Is it? Quite the contrary. I would urge that it is precisely this situation which makes consideration of the church, its form and its reform, an urgent necessity. For we must realize that we are not only reaching the eschaton, but that it has revealed itself as essentially an eschaton in human relationships. We *have* to become reconciled to each other or destroy ourselves. Science has brought us face to face with our own nature. We either meet that challenge or risk the extinction of our race. Scientific knowledge and moral advancement ought to have kept pace with each other. They have not, and that is our basic tragedy. We can be certain of one thing: if we try, with our present degree of scientific expertise, to solve our social and political problems on the basis of the old power plays — revolutionary or traditionalist — we shall have forfeited our right as a race to continue, or we will continue only in a brutalized form. Is it an accident that we have reached this threshold at a time when all our most pressing human problems can be solved only in community with others? Population control, problems of the environment, worldwide poverty and national affluence, crime and violence, and above all war — all are problems that involve the total human community and demand the readiness of human beings to become reconciled to each other.

Reconciliation — which must never be confused with mere compromise — is at the heart of it; and if that is true we cannot ignore the community that was brought into being to demonstrate what that should mean. But equally if that is true, the enormity of the church's failure stands clear, and its awful responsibility for the plight of the world that Christ came to save.

Notes to Chapter 3

1 *On Revolution* (New York: Viking, 1968), p. 30; cf. p. 2.

2 Letter to Richard Mayor, August 13, 1649.

3 Leslie Cooke, *Bread and Laughter* (Geneva: WCC, 1968), p. 265.

4 *United Church Herald,* July 1, 1969, p. 3; italics added.

5 We must carefully distinguish between what is politically possible in South America, Asia and Africa and what is viable in the world's technocracies. The appearance of a "theology of Liberation," associated with such names as Gustavo Gutierrez and Rubem Alves, suggests that revolution in the classical sense may still be a live option in the former (cf. Gustavo Gutierrez, *A Theology of Liberation,* 1973, and the debate in the Sept. 17th and Oct. 15th issues of *Christianity and Crisis* in 1973). It is clear that the social inequities in South America are causing a ferment in the churches of that continent at this time. On the other hand, the very urgency of the writings may reflect the fear that the time for effective action is rapidly running out.

6 *The Church Inside Out* (Philadelphia: Westminster, 1964), p. 48.

7 Reported by Eileen Sander, *Saturday Review,* June 28, 1969,

pp. 46f.; italics added. Lennon repeated the same point in a television interview conducted by David Frost, July 10, 1969.

8 "Relevance: the Shadow of a Magnitude," *Daedalus*, Summer 1969, p. 657; italics added.

9 See "My Classmate the Enemy," *Newsweek*, December 20, 1971, p. 38.

10 Compare Louis XIV's policy toward the Huguenots, Elizabeth I's persecution of the Puritans, and the Puritans' attempts to keep their theocracy pure in New England.

11 The obvious exceptions were the "Glorious Revolution" of England in 1688 and the American Revolution. Of the former, Eugen Rosenstock-Huessey justly commented that it was neither glorious nor a revolution; and the latter shares the characteristics of a civil war as much as those of a revolution: nor was it a revolution in the social sense that would be true of the French or Russian revolutions.

12 A government built on a totalitarian principle may become more liberal with the years, but we have to notice how it reacts when the dissent begins to threaten its own existence. White power in South Africa was, for example, more liberal for a time under Smuts, but it has become increasingly a police state. Similarly we note how the USSR reacted to the threat in Hungary (1956), in Czechoslovakia (1968), and to the threat posed by its own intellectuals (Yuli M. Daniel and Andrei D. Sinyavsky in 1966; and Aleksandr Solzhenitsyn, Pyotr Yakir, Andrei Amalrik, and others in 1973). Of course, no government will flout world opinion gratuitously, particularly since the stakes are high; but there can be no doubt that wherever the means to suppress dissent exists, it will not be tolerated beyond a certain point.

13 Occasional articles appear in the popular press on this subject, but the question of who is to exercise the control has hardly received the popular exposure that the issue warrants. Closely related to genetic control is the "new embryology"; cf. *Newsweek*, November 22, 1970, p. 120.

14 Some of the political implications are commented on in the article on which this chapter is based, "Violent Revolution is Obsolete," *Presbyterian Life*, January 1, 1970.

Chapter 4

Between Scylla and Charybdis

> My grandfather and I
> Go walking in the rain
>   and thinking.
> I can tell that he's remembering,
> His face seems softer and so far away.
> There's a space between us as we walk
> And though he will not notice it —
> I can feel it's always there.

— Vicki Druss (age 13), *McCall's*, February 1970

How shall we claim a respectful hearing from you? The usual complaint of the old about the young might well be reversed today. . . . In many matters it will be almost impossible for you to establish any link with the past. I wonder if you realise what a privilege that is, however? . . . Let me tell you that it is a mark of distinction for a younger generation to be forced to accept the freedom of individual responsibility as you are today—perhaps for the first time for a very long age in the history of the relationship between young and old.

— Karl Barth, in talks given to Hungarian youth, 1948

As they neared the coast of Sicily, the sailors of the ancient world knew that they would have to navigate between the twin horrors of Scylla and Charybdis, and the danger was that in avoiding the one they would fall afoul of the other.

The danger of our present-day polarization between young and old is like that. Each understands and discerns very clearly a danger that is real, but I suggest the very clarity with which we have seen the danger that is real to our own generation prevents us from appreciating the warnings that come from the other side. Our technological civilization has created a whole series of problems that threaten to swamp us, but the ultimate political danger presents a double threat that forces us to steer between the Scylla of totalitarian war with its possibility of nuclear annihilation, and the Charybdis of totalitarian control with its equal possibility of dehumanization.

If it were simply a case of avoiding the one or the other, there would be no problem, no talk of national disunity, no crazy mixed-up situation in which men of obvious integrity feel it necessary to commit acts of sabotage against the state to protest their higher loyalty and men of equal loyalty to the truth as they see it defend repression and acts of incredible barbarism. There is no doubt that the tension between the generations experienced in the 1960s was a worldwide phenomenon, but because of the simple idealism that other peoples had come to expect of America and because of its unique commitments, it was in the United States that the polarization received its most dramatic expression. It remains, I suggest, because both dangers are real.

If the enemy had a single face, the people would readily fall in behind their chosen leaders to meet it. Society would be able to regain that single-minded purpose that gives national and ideological unity and turns any nation into a happy company of crusaders. But the threat is a double threat, and the real danger in the present situation is the polarization that hinders us from recognizing the complex reality as it is. In our situation yearning for the unambiguous unity that was known in the past could be a positive menace.

We are looking for a new concept of social solidarity that will enable us to reach unity through a diversity of opinions. For perhaps the hardest lesson we have to learn is that the old politics will no longer do. In the past a national policy that was able to opt for one side of a simple alternative and to marshall the full strength of a nation behind it by suppressing or ridiculing dissent was the surest way of achieving national unity and often of winning the national goals. Today it can no longer guarantee unity and may be the surest way to communal destruction. We may have to learn not only how to live with our differences but also how to defend them. Certainly in international politics we shall have to recognize that the attempt to reconcile opposing positions is the only policy that can take the place of war.

So, too, in the concerns of a single people. We have to recognize the legitimate convictions on both sides of the generation gap, for in steering between Scylla and Charybdis one cannot afford to ignore either.

* * *

Obviously, since 1945 the immediate menace has been the possibility of total destruction through the hydrogen bomb or one of its horrendous rivals. It is not important whether annihilation comes through the bomb or biological warfare, whether it is delivered through conventional bombers, missiles, or satellites. The threat is the same, and it is certainly the threat that is most real to the generations that have grown up since Hiroshima.

That we have lived with this threat for a quarter of a century without its happening is scant comfort: the potential clearly exists and it needs to happen only once.

It is difficult for the middle-aged to understand what this means. If those who became adults before that historical climacteric would reflect a little longer on what this means to their sons and daughters and to every little child on the street, they might have more understanding. We have had to live with it; they were born with it. Deeper reflection might enable us to see the young — whether college radicals, war protesters, or black militants, whether unwashed demonstrators or deodorized exponents of the "new morality" — as persons who deserve our compassion rather than our hatred. These young people face an unprecedented human dilemma, which they did not create and did not ask to enter. There is some justification for thinking that the wisdom of previous generations will not automatically solve their problems for them. The threats they discern to the security of the race are real enough and they are predominantly the results of what has happened in the twentieth century.

This post-World War II generation may have so little time. And that nuclear threat — in the sense that it has been presented indiscriminately at birth to everyone throughout the world who was born since August 6, 1945 — makes this generation different from any previous one in the world's history. Other peoples have faced doom — the chances of a baby born in Germany during the Thirty Years' War or of a Jewish family in the time of Hitler were not very high — but never before has the doom hung over the whole race. This circumstance of their birthdate unites young Americans with their erstwhile enemies in Japan; it unites the young people of the West with those from whom they are supposed to be ideologically separated in Russia or China. They haven't the time to be patient. As one young poet from East Germany expresses it in his poem "To Old Comrades":

> The present, for you
> A sweet goal after all those bitter years
> Is for me a bitter beginning, and
> Calls for changes. Full of impatience
> I hurl myself into the battle. . . .
> And therefore, with my impatience
> Don't be impatient, old men. . . . [1]

How can we counsel patience to those who may have so little time left? It is easy enough to offer caution and to advise patience and moderation to those who look forward to a broad future of possibility — any kind of future. But the young to whom we offer our advice know that they may not have the future we have always assumed; and since the world of our past mistakes is all around them, we cannot blame them for their skepticism about our promises. They want peace, human dignity, and the possibility of celebrating the joy of being alive, which is their birthright. And they want it now.

Nobel Prizewinner George Wald put the issue for youth very well in an address delivered in spring 1969, "A Generation in Search of a Future."[2] Dr. Wald said that he has become increasingly aware that something has gone wrong in the relation between the teacher and the taught, "almost as though there were a widespread feeling that education has become irrelevant." Setting himself the task of finding out what was the root cause of his students' discontent and uneasiness, he went on to say:

I think I know what is bothering the students. I think that what we are up against is a generation that is by no means sure that it has a future.

I am growing old, and my future, so to speak, is already behind me. But there are those students of mine, who are in my mind always; and there are my children, the youngest of them now seven and nine, whose future is infinitely

61

more precious to me than my own. So it isn't just their generation; it's mine too. We're all in it together.

Are we to have a chance to live? We don't ask for prosperity, or security. Only for a reasonable chance to live, to work out our destiny in peace and decency. Not to go down in history as the apocalyptic generation.

And it isn't only nuclear war. Another overwhelming threat is in the population explosion. That has not yet even begun to come under control. . . .

That is the problem. Unless we can be surer than we are now that this generation has a future, nothing else matters. It's not good enough to give it tender, loving care, to supply it with breakfast foods, to buy it expensive educations. Those things don't mean anything unless this generation has a future. And we are not sure that it has.

This is where the generation gap begins, for how can the majority of us who lived through the earlier years of this century, with all of our bland ideas about human progress and our expectation of a virtually limitless future, really comprehend that *the future may not take place*; that, indeed, in view of what we know about human nature and scientific probability, the chances of man's survival far into the next century are extremely remote? How can we who come from a world of historically conditioned traditions understand that? How can we grasp the fact that our culture and all we have regarded as permanent, the writing, art, music, science, and philosophy—the whole corporate memory of the race—may go up in one enormous mushroom cloud, or disappear with T. S. Eliot's apocalyptic whimper as life flickers out in global famine? It is unthinkable, impossible for us to imagine, and so, because it has not yet happened, it is easier to think that it will not. But neither our inability to comprehend it nor the fact that it has not happened makes it any less likely. We come from a time when the future was real, when the possibilities for any people were largely guaranteed by its readiness to support its leaders, to fight for its rights against invaders or oppressors, to work steadily to build on the past, and to obey the moral law that had been handed down. These were the tried and trusted ways by which societies had guaranteed their own survival up to the present. Until the total threat became visible in 1945 and became the sinister canopy under which the new generation was born, nothing could challenge the claims of tradition, for tradition had worked successfully, at least in bringing the race (nation, tribe, family) to that point in history. This success vested in respect for the past goes a long way to explain the reason why societies reacted so slowly to innovation, and why revolution was regarded with universal horror until comparatively modern times.

Those of us born before 1945 were born into societies where this respect for the past was still possible and even justifiable, because it still offered a future. How then can we fully understand the sweet bitterness of our children, to whom the past has become largely meaningless, the future a question mark, and who insist on writing the whole of their lives in terms of the present imperative? To bring this generation to birth is one thing, but to bring it to birth with this unwanted legacy was to raise a radical question mark against the whole sweep of history by which we had reached that point in time. By putting the future in issue, we placed the past under indictment. Moreover, we have been gradually coming to realize since 1945 that the dropping of the atomic bomb on Hiroshima was only symptomatic, and that the advent of nuclear fission only underlined more insistently a doom that we were bringing on the race by the whole trend of our acquisitive technological culture.

In a graphic and widely publicized illustration Margaret Mead has pointed to the essential difference between the generations. "What's happening now is an immigration in time, with the people over 40 the migrants into the present age and the children born in it the natives. The world the youth are in tune with and take for granted is different from the world of their elders, and the children who have grown up in the space age understand things out of their continuous experience that adults have to learn."[3] Her words have been given even more point by the writings of Marshall McLuhan and the recognition that a whole generation was growing up whose ideas, standards, and mores had been largely shaped by the mass media, which the rest of us still regarded as the clever playthings of our affluent society.

The protest of the young against the domination of the past has a crystal clarity and an immediacy we cannot escape. Every civilization and society has developed its own mythology and used it to establish its power among the people. Societies appeal not to the truth but to as much of the truth as fits in with their own "ideal" picture of themselves. In this sense truth has always been a very flexible commodity, depending on how much could be assimilated by the wise men and seers, how much could be used by the politicians and men of affairs, and how much could be accepted and incorporated into the general world-view that the society or nation held at the time. Most people tacitly recognized that within any prevailing mythology there would be little lies and little hypocrisies, but these were not held to be too significant as long as the overall "truth" of the mythology was accepted and supported the society's goals. There was not much to question it, because the pragmatic answer appeared to be unassailable: "Of course we have problems! Of course there are faults and inaccuracies! But don't knock the system, for at least it has prevented us from falling prey to foreign enemies or to the inner rot of anarchy." There was no answer to that because however dark the immediate future appeared, there was a future and it always seemed to have light in it for some.

In their protest the young of our time have an advantage (if that is what it should be called) over all their predecessors, because that which threatens our race undercuts this basic argument by the absoluteness of the doom it offers and the comprehensiveness of its scope. We have arrived at this point by means of the very historical processes that up to now have been claimed to guarantee man's survival. We have reached the nemesis, and the clear-eyed young point out to us that this is the logical result of civilizations that allowed life and progress to be founded on lies, half-truths, exaggerations, hypocrisies, and untruths carefully hidden even from those using them. We have become the victims of our own web-spinning. They declare, with a good deal of justification, that because we live in times that are wholly unprecedented, the lessons of the past are less likely to provide us with sound answers than to lead us awry. They claim that they are a new generation, prepared to be completely honest about life as it is, looking for a new morality based on openness and honesty to everyone and in all relationships, and new forms of education in which the responses of teaching and learning may be mutually shared by all who are involved in it. And we have to listen, because one of the things that the younger generation understands better than we can — with our national conditioning and sectional interests — is the total togetherness of all life and the urgency of the present time in view of the tragic threat that covers us all.

* * *

There is another side to the picture. We are menaced not only by the possibility of mass annihilation but also by the possibility of coming completely under the control of a system and thus becoming dehumanized. Totalitarian government becomes a greater danger in this respect as science and technology provide more and more instruments with which to control, change, and mold the individuality of persons. I am not raising anew the Russian bogey of the 1950s or the Chinese bogey of the 1960s or suggesting we invent any other bogey for the 1970s. I am referring to any soulless system prepared to drive for its own goals by ruthlessly suppressing all that makes its citizens human. In this respect I find the benevolent social engineering of B. F. Skinner's utopia *Walden II* perhaps more frightening, because more plausible, than Aldous Huxley's *Brave New World* or George Orwell's *1984*. In any case, who is to say that those who gain control will be benevolent, or that we would agree with the meaning they give to the term? Any technically advanced state probably now has the means to achieve this kind of controlled society. If those who govern are ruthless enough, 1984 could become a reality at any date.

There was a time — perhaps in the 1930s — when this would have been regarded as practically out of the question. We might have conceded that the technical ability would become available at some time in the future, for we had seen the effect of the "truth drugs" at the Moscow trials of 1936-38, but most people would have doubted whether any nation in "Christendom" would be ruthless enough to crush absolutely all individual freedom and initiative. One of the reasons why "godless Russia" was so abhorred in the West during the Stalin era was that her government evidenced a good deal of this kind of ruthlessness.

Then came Hitler, and trickling out of Germany there were the rumors of the systematic genocide of the Jews. Six million of our fellow human beings were systematically slaughtered. We witnessed the deportation of whole populations into slave labor, mass executions such as that at Lidice, and obscenities that we did not believe possible in the twentieth century. We learned too a good deal about the deliberate distortion of truth, and about the weakness of many liberal institutions when under relentless pressure. The possibility that a nation could come under the control of a degenerate clique and be mobilized to bring about the enslavement of humanity was no longer to be dismissed as a nightmare dreamed by sensation-hungry journalists. The possibility — even the probability — for such a regime to be successful was plain for all to see. From that point of view we were fortunate by comparison with the modern generation, for the Second World War was at least clear-cut: those who lived through it in Europe do not doubt that if Hitler had won, death might have been preferable.

Those who fought in that beautifully unambiguous war see the possibility that this threat may rise again to haunt mankind. And they are right, for it is a real threat. Our children do not know what an Auschwitz, a Belsen, a Buchenwald can do to human dignity, for Hitler is old history, part of the past they never experienced. They do not see in the New Left and the New Right (and at many points in between) the obscene potential for the kind of world that Hitler stood for. Lord Acton's aphorism, "Power corrupts, and absolute power corrupts absolutely," may sound platitudinous, but the history of revolution gives it almost one hundred percent support. We cannot blame young people for being less willing to risk death on a global scale than they are to risk totalitarianism on a global scale, but we do ask them to try to understand the legitimate fears that their parents bring from the past.

To catch the mood of the older generation one need

make only a few changes in the illustration cited above from Margaret Mead. There *is* a real sense in which today's young people are like the "natives" of a new world within which their parents can be no more than immigrants. But those same parents have some excuse for thinking of the situation rather differently. To them it seems that they were the simple "natives" who have welcomed into their midst the young, ruthless agents of a totally alien culture and now find, like the original inhabitants of America, that their own culture has been ruthlessly subjugated and taken over by a stronger one that rides on the wave of the future.

* * *

One of the circumstances of our time that pushes the polarization of the generations further is that all the threats to the future — nuclear war, population explosion and world famine, and land, sea, and air poisoned by the effluents of our affluence—are problems that have little hope of being solved unless we are willing to act as a unified world community. They demand giving up of national sovereignty and accepting international control and wide executive planning. These are dirty words to fathers and mothers brought up on the simple creeds of Americanism, the Monroe Doctrine, and opposition to the New Deal.

On the other hand it should be clear to us, whether we are conservative or radical, young or old, that these issues raised here are basically moral ones. They involve reconciliation — of people to people, class to class, nation to nation — and how far we can expect elected representatives to act responsibly in the exercise of the unprecedented powers that this kind of government demands. The next "great step for mankind," beyond space exploration and technical achievements, must be ethical; indeed, it cannot be political unless it is first ethical, for the old politics of power have gone as far as they can, and we see the result.

The generations must bridge the gap in their understanding of each other by taking each other's fears with complete seriousness. George Wald is absolutely right: "We're all in it together." For that reason the polarities, the "either . . . or" thinking forced on us by the old politics, will not do. Humanity has to become reconciled enough to be able to search for its answers in community, for the one thing that we should fear more than any other in the present struggle is the kind of absolute victory that will allow one side to impose its solutions and priorities on the other. As I have argued in a previous chapter, this is particularly true in the threat of revolution within our Western society; for although it appears to offer spectacular and immediate results, it could end by destroying us all. And those who would be most destroyed would be those who assumed they were to be its predestined victors.

To become reconciled to our neighbor is no longer a liberal sentiment to be brought out with the plastic angels at Christmas time. It is the basic necessity of our continued existence as a race. Reconciliation is our ultimate need because the time for dogmatic absolutes has passed. If we doubt the solutions and the motives of the other person, we can neither be any longer so sure of our own. We need the corrective wisdom of each other, and in no area is this more needed than in that which separates the generations.

There is an almost painful aptness to the warning and promise with which the Old Testament ends. In foretelling the coming of the prophet Elijah, who would be the precursor of the kingdom of God, Malachi said that "he will turn the hearts of the fathers to their children and the hearts of the children to their fathers, lest I come and smite the land with a curse" (Mal. 4:5).

Isn't it odd that this is the point where the old covenant ends, and the new covenant can be expected to begin?

Notes to Chapter 4

1 Wolf Biermann, *The Wire Harp*, tr. Eric Bentley (New York: Harcourt, Brace & World, 1967), pp. 69-70.

2 Delivered at the Massachusetts Institute of Technology, March 4, 1969; as reported in *The New Yorker*, March 22, 1969.

3 As quoted in *This Week*, September 29, 1968, p. 2.

Chapter 5

The Reconciling Community

Nothing can arrest the judgment of the Cross, nothing shake the judgment-seat of Christ. The world gets a long time to pay, but all the accounts are kept — to the uttermost farthing. Lest if anything were forgotten there might be something unforgiven, unredeemed, and unholy still.

P. T. Forsyth, *The Justification of God*

The only divine Lord of the world is He who does not wish to rule it, but to bless it by way of service.

P. T. Forsyth, *The Church and the Sacraments*

We need not postpone the basic issue any longer, for we can now put the question of the church's relevance in a clearer context. We are pushed back to the simple truism from Shakespeare's *Julius Caesar*: "The fault, dear Brutus, is not in our stars but in ourselves, that we are underlings." The problem between the generations, between the races, between social and economic classes,[1] between opposing cultures and ideologies is the problem of reconciliation. Indeed, the women's liberation movement reminds us that we might have had the same ongoing warfare between the sexes, had we not been forced

71

by simple laws of biology to recognize that at least at this primary level a form of love is the only guarantee of our survival as a race.

The lesson of our apocalyptic age is that humanity is destroying itself because we have become alienated from each other, from our own true nature, and—perhaps most fundamentally of all—from that which (or from the one who) called us into being, gives us a sense of destiny, and is responsible for our experience of "grace." The competitive and belligerent drives that may have served well enough in a more primitive state are now dangerously obsolete, and we shall either learn to control them or destroy ourselves in the hatreds of irreconcilable ideologies and racial resentments. Any purely pragmatic assessment of our chances for survival shows that we will either learn the lesson of reconciliation or join the other discards of history.

For want of language any more pertinent to our own situation we echo a comment made about churches in the first decade of this century, when it was said that "the note of judgment has gone out of modern piety."[2] Now judgment enters our world again, not as the executioner from some myth of the dark ages, not as the tragic finale in a traditional orthodoxy, not because the righteous can gloat over it or sadistically revel in the prospect of a holocaust from which they are somehow excluded, but because it is written into what our race is making of itself.

We have to take note again of sin, not as the sum of little peccadilloes, but the sin of the whole race, social as well as individual, what Forsyth called sin solidary. This is something we can no longer explain away and say it does not matter, or use as an excuse for crime in the streets or in the hallways of the Pentagon; for we see that beyond all the social conditioning that has helped to produce it, it is a matter of will to which we have all contributed. It is not from our moral lapses nor from our individual taint that we need to be delivered, "but from world sin, sin in dominion, sin solidary if not hereditary, yea, from sin which integrates us into a Satanic Kingdom."[3]

That note has to come back into the Christian proclamation, the authentic note of urgency that was heard in the New Testament. It was said that "we have churches of the nicest, kindest people, who have nothing apostolic or missionary, who never knew the soul's despair or its breathless gratitude."[4] It can no longer be charged that the message of judgment preys on men's selfish fear of damnation in some distant world beyond time. That can take care of itself, and everyone can make up his own mind about it. But judgment is *here*, in this present world and in our own time, whatever our theological beliefs or unbeliefs. Here is a gospel of urgency that the church can proclaim with some hope of being understood by our contemporaries. More than that, it is a gospel we are charged to proclaim, for at this point we are not preaching from some safe position outside the common experience of our fellows. The condemnation for our failure to be reconciled begins with the church: quite literally, like Richard Baxter, we preach "as a dying man to dying men."

To stumble into religious conformity through fear of what may happen to one's own soul is an act of cowardice, and, if it implies salvation at the expense of other poor unfortunates, an act of callous selfishness. As Bonhoeffer pointed out, to conform to religious beliefs because of such fears is also an act of weakness and immaturity. The judgment we proclaim here is different. Flagrantly to pursue my own selfish ends when the results of what I do involve not only my own destruction but the destruction of all that is human is not an act of brave maturity but of selfish immaturity and recklessness. If our world has really become "adult" and takes responsibility for its own decisions in the way Bonhoeffer suggested, it must begin to look at its own situation realistically. Perhaps, too, it will take the risk of turning back on its own history, turning away from the old politics based on distrust and force, and accept the adventure of reconciliation.

* * *

How then can a community that has the proclamation and exemplification of reconciliation at its heart be irrelevant? If the church has the proclamation and demonstration of reconciliation in community as its very *raison d'être*, there is little in our society that should speak more relevantly to the human condition. If reconciliation is at the center of the church's life and meaning, it would be folly to ignore the church.

But to describe the church as a community that has the proclamation and demonstration of reconciliation as the reason for its existence is to reveal an enormous gap between theory and practice. We have to accept the fact that the gap exists, and then work with all other people of goodwill to close it. The irrelevance of the church to many of the deepest concerns of its own members is the irrelevance of what "the churches" have made of "the church," and not of what the church itself is supposed to be. The point of alienation is the point at which there appears to be almost total unrelatedness between the actual and the ideal; for in common honesty we have to admit that, divided and proscribed by its denominational absolutes, the church has often become the very opposite of a reconciling community. Church history reveals that in hatred and hostility toward each other the churches have often instructed the powers of this world in the finer arts of arrogance and demonic cruelty. This has sometimes approached the ultimate blasphemy when they have claimed to do these things under the influence of Christ's own spirit. Even today, in the way its power structures operate, in maintaining attitudes of racial segregation (both white and black),[5] in class consciousness, in the suburban churches' incredible insensitivity to the desperate needs of others, the church is a denial of reconciliation in word and deed.

No one should interpret this criticism in purely Protestant or Catholic terms. As I write reports of bombings in Northern Ireland continue. Yesterday's newspaper carried a picture of a Protestant father crying at the funeral of his son; a few days earlier there was a picture of a Catholic mother at her daughter's funeral. This is the church's history, and we are all involved in it — Catholic and Protestant alike. We can no longer wash our hands of the more inconvenient parts of church history with pleas like, "This was not done by *my* church; it was the Catholics," or "See how those barbarous Protestants treated poor old Ireland!" It is all church history, the history of institutions that profess to serve the same Jesus Christ I profess to serve. Perhaps our testimony will truly begin only as the churches recognize their own solidarity in sin and penitence.

Reconciliation is at the heart of the church's meaning, and because that is so the church, even when it is most apostate, has within it a dynamic of self-criticism that it can never entirely ignore. It is this miraculous possibility of self-criticism, re-creation, and renewal that springs from the gospel itself which prevents us from discarding the church. This was illustrated by the explanation a young man recently gave for his decision to enter the parish ministry. "Ministry for Hosea began with marriage: 'Go marry a whore, and get children with a whore, for this country has become nothing but a whore by abandoning Yahweh.' For me to marry a whore and get children by her means accepting responsibility with the

75

church for what she has been (we share a mutual and cowardly disobedience) and committing myself to the future to which we are called by God."[6] Despite the faint scent of the Pharisee in that statement, I know what is meant. We can make no more claims for the church in terms of power, status, or holiness, for from the side of man the church is *never* perfect; and she always manifests a witness that is ambiguous and set within the mixed motives and competing ambitions of our human lot.

But we should not only be concerned about the church as it is. We must also strive for what it was intended to be—a human fellowship in which there was to be no distinction between "Jew or Greek, slave and free man, male or female," where all were to be one in Christ (Gal. 3:28; cf. Col. 3:11).[7] This is the very essence of the church, to proclaim and exemplify reconciliation; and it is centered in Jesus Christ. "What I mean," says the apostle, "is that God in Christ was reconciling the world to himself, no longer counting men's misdeeds against them, and that he has entrusted us with the message of reconciliation" (II Cor. 5:18-19).

Beyond the question of Atonement—the "at-one-ment" Jesus achieved for his people—the reconciliation about which this passage speaks has social dimensions.

In the first place, if we are true to the spirit of the New Testament, we see that the gospel is validated by the character of those who proclaim it. The testimony of the Holy Spirit speaks through both the proclamation and the one who proclaims. Just as the message of Jesus was validated by the quality of his life, so the life and character of the community entrusted with the gospel are intended to witness to the truth that is being proclaimed.[8]

The New Testament does not allow theology to be divorced from ethics. This is made very clear in the summary of the law that Jesus quoted: "The first [commandment] is, 'Hear, O Israel: the Lord your God is the only Lord; love the Lord your God with all your heart, with all your soul, with all your mind, and with all your strength. The second is this: 'Love your neighbor as yourself.' There is no other commandment greater than these" (Mark 12:29-32; cf. Matt. 22:37-40). According to Luke, the story of the Good Samaritan was told as a direct and pertinent commentary for those who might wish to set national or ecclesiastical boundaries to this ethical imperative (Luke 10:27-37). What is more to the point, it gives a practical demonstration of what reconciliation demands of us: we are to meet human need wherever it is to be found. There is to be no separation between theology and ethics; for "if a man says 'I love God,' while hating his brother, he is a liar. If he does not love the brother whom he has seen, it cannot be that he loves God whom he has not seen. And indeed this command comes to us from Christ himself: that he who loves God must also love his brother" (I John 4:20f.). The great contribution of Christian activism over the past decade has been to recognize the central place that this occupies in the gospel, and to stimulate the church to recognize it.

Secondly, when we speak of reconciliation as the essence of the church, we cannot ignore that this is entrusted to a community. Paul obviously had the Christian fellowship in mind; and if a community is to be more than a mere aggregate of like-minded individuals brought casually together for *ad hoc* purposes, it will presumably be established with a given form that sufficiently declares its nature and purpose or seek forms to express its essential nature and structures to serve its purpose truly. Most of the older theologies of the church had no doubt that the form had been given, claiming for themselves an origin exclusively *de jure divino*; and the others fell into difficulties of their own (which are discussed at greater length in *The Church in Search of Its Self*). If this ministry of atonement, reconciliation, belongs to the essence of the church, and if the church exists to represent this gospel in corporate, communal terms to the world, we are forced to ask how the church can begin to do this in Christ's name without radically reforming the present structures that proclaim its own inner disunity.

In this context we cannot ignore the ecumenical movement, for it has thrown the brightest spotlight on the meaning of the church in this century. One often finds sympathetic critics of the church — even those who should know better — speaking as if the movement has been born out of the churches' present embarrassments. One such critic recently observed that "no doubt the ecumenical movement will be stimulated by this sense of corporate weakness, but it is unlikely that unity brought about on such a basis will prove either enduring or a source of additional strength—rather, if anything, the reverse."[9]

True. All intelligent and experienced ecumenists would agree with that: they have been saying it for about fifty years. The ecumenical movement did not arise out of despondency and despair in the churches, but out of expansion and tremendous optimism. It was called into being by the churches not to meet the threat of doom, but to take full advantage of the evangelical opportunities opening up to them. It was born not in the churches' weakness, but in their strength. It was in 1910, during the heyday of British Free Church optimism, that the International Missionary Conference was called at Edinburgh specifically to discuss the relationship of the churches to each other in the areas of Christian mission. The step was unprecedented, because it was the first time the churches had recognized each other on a representative basis. From this one conference the movements developed that brought the World Council of Churches into being in 1948. However much the ecumenical movement may be stimulated at present by the practical concern of economy and conservation, at its inception it was inspired by the missionary conviction that the churches cannot proclaim reconciliation to the rest of the world until they have the integrity to do something about their own dividedness: if the time has come for the judgment, "it is beginning with God's own household" (I Peter 4:17).[10]

Something similar appears to be true of the ecumenical concern in Roman Catholicism. Whatever the practical reasons that led John XXIII to call Roman Catholics to an *aggiornamento*, the spontaneous gesture of reaching out to other Christians seems to have come from a man of genuine pastoral character and unusual sensitivity, and the response since Vatican II shows the extent to which his concern was shared by others in the church. It is also clear that the inspiration for the ecumenical movement in the Roman Catholic Church arose from a genuine return to Scripture and the theology of renewal. As soon as the historic revelation is taken seriously by Catholic, Protestant, and Orthodox, the question of reconciliation among Christians themselves can no longer be avoided: to face the church's mission as the reconciling community raises first the need of the churches to let themselves be reconciled.

I am convinced that the search for Christian unity, and specifically our attempts to translate that unity into terms of ecclesiastical union, far from being desperate attempts to postpone disaster, are imperatives from the gospel itself; for before we can proclaim reconciliation effectively in the world we must show that we ourselves are reconciled. Furthermore, although the spirit of unity in the church is primary, the form of unity in the church cannot be ignored, because that form itself should be a witness to the church's message of reconciliation.

* * *

Here I revert to Margaret Mead's illustration cited in the last chapter. Whether one thinks of the older generation as immigrants entering a foreign culture or as native "Indians" being overrun by an alien culture will largely depend, I suspect, on one's own age and attitude to history. But if we older people are immigrants, it is of a particular sort, for we cannot help also entering it as missionaries.

Presumably some will be missionaries of that irrelevant and pernicious kind that tries to coerce the "natives" into accepting old-time answers just because these are the answers with which they themselves have lived and feel most comfortable. But it is to be hoped that some of us will be missionaries of a new style—strangers perhaps, but shyly offering friendship; prepared to share our faith with others, while remaining always open and in dialogue with a culture that we recognize as different from our own. We will try to identify with this new society and its inhabitants without making any arrogant claims that we can ever wholly belong.

Good or bad, we cannot help being missionaries of some sort. Those of us who profess the Christian faith have a responsibility to witness that comes from the very nature of that faith. We are missionaries primarily to our own children, testifying that there *is* a place for hope even when faith seems hardly possible, that as long as there is hope there can be a future, and that the faith that has sustained us has this promise at its heart. We are also missionaries bearing witness that as one gets older and faces the inevitability of death, he begins to understand that the eschaton has been on our own individual doorstep all the time—that even as hope stretches wider than the individual consciousness, so it may have deeper springs than the corporate memory or fate of our race. We testify to the conviction that beyond all that we have done or could do, we have been upheld by something that is inexplicable but which may be best described as pure grace; and we point to the insight that if you would find an ultimate meaning in life you must go beyond reason to discover God, because he refuses to coerce you even through your intelligence.

The quality of this missionary vocation has come to us largely because of an encounter with a single human personality. He is the one who epitomizes all we would wish to say to our children, and of whom it has been said, in the words of someone who admits he started late in his missionary vocation, that "Though in terms of history, the darkness falls, blacking out us and our world, You have overcome history. You came as Light into the world, that whoever believed in You should not remain in darkness. The promise stands forever."[11] We are witnesses to this, and *because* we are witnesses to this faith we have also to testify to the community of those who have shared the same encounter, and who, in a stumbling way, have been trying to make real in terms of human community the reconciliation that Jesus offered to men.

"The chief problem with the church is not in the world but in itself."[12] It has always been so—since the time when it carried in its midst Thomas the doubter, Peter the apostate, and Judas the traitor. All of the disciples were cowards who ran away at the time of testing; and if there is any fundamental difference between them and the traitor Judas, it was only that they remained to receive Christ's forgiveness. When naturally irreligious people turn their backs on the church with the comment that the members of the church are "all hypocrites," I can understand what they are rejecting even though I cannot accept the moral snobbery that this attitude implies: the sin of Lucifer is no more attractive among secularists than it has been among the devout.

But the criticism is just. The church never has been anything but a community of sinners standing in the need of grace; and it was never in greater danger of apostasy than when it forgot that and began to strut around the world certain of its own election. Indeed, there never has been a time when the church could claim any holiness of its own, and it can claim no holiness at all apart from that which was given to it in the good news that "God was in Christ reconciling the world to himself." Wherever we look in the New Testament we are directed away from the human instruments that carry the message to the one who personified the message: "so the Word became flesh; and he came to dwell among us, and we saw his glory, such glory as befits the Father's only Son, full of grace and truth" (John 1:14, NEB). The church is the community testimony of those who in the brightness of this revelation of God's grace have been brought to their knees, acknowledged their own spiritual need, and try to respond to the commission, "Rise to your feet and stand upright. I have appeared to you for a purpose: to appoint you my servant and witness, to testify to what you have seen, and to what you shall yet see of me" (Acts 26:16, NEB).

For Saul of Tarsus this was a commission given to him as an individual, and throughout church history there have been those who have heard and obeyed a similar imperative charge to dedicate themselves to a life of witness. But Christians have not recognized as readily that if the church has any significance it is to make this testimony *corporate*. Far beyond being a congregation of disciples, or even a missionary society of individual apostles, it has the unique task of making the at-one-ment which Jesus revealed in his life, death, and resurrection objectively real in terms of human community. Reconciliation is the very reason for its existence, and it is a reconciliation that cannot be proclaimed effectively from pulpits until it is first lived and demonstrated in the tensions and joys of a community prepared to make that kind of witness in the conditions of this world.

Jesus showed men that it is possible to be human in this world and revealed the quality of human life that the Creator had intended. The church's special task is to show men that it is also possible to live humanly as a society of humans, and the whole creation has groaned until now as it has waited to see what the adoption of the sons of God would be like. Written in large letters over our human condition, the message of our time seems to be that if the gospel cannot be made corporate and translated into communal human forms, it is no gospel for our race. Reconciliation has to be made real and demonstrated to be real at that existential point before the church will begin to accomplish her mission, or before twentieth-century men will feel inclined to listen.

That is why judgment has to begin with the household of God, and that is why the nature of the church we present to men and the shape of the church we adopt among men cannot be irrelevant. P. T. Forsyth pointed in this direction in some comments about the church (which occur almost as an aside in one of his books). Arguing for flexibility in the interpretation of the Scriptures, he pointed out that the gospel means something done rather than simply declared, and that this deed was the purpose of our Lord's coming. Then he went on to say, "And to give this work effect Bible and Church

83

alike exist. We treat the Church as plastic to its fulfilment, do we not? That is the true Church, and the true form of the Church, which gives best effect to the Gospel."[13] Forsyth saw that the form the church takes in this world depends on its essential mission. I would push it even further—that what the church *does* and, much more fundamentally, what it *is* are the constantly broadcast commentary on how much faith the church has in its own gospel.

So we are back at the point from which we began. The pressures of our age, the storms brewing in the churches themselves, and the secular hurricanes threatening to engulf it do not force us to push the doctrine of the church to one side or to regard it as irrelevant. Rather, they force us to sound a note of almost desperate urgency that the nature of the church and its shape in this world should be a matter of imperative ecumenical concern, because our human condition tells us that at many urgent levels the things that threaten human survival center in the unsolved problems of our human relationships. We need desperately to become at-oned, reconciled, with our destiny in creation, with our own nature, with each other, and with all the creatures who share this earth with us. And the church was called into being to show what that kind of community would mean. It points to the kingdom of God.

Notes to Chapter 5

1 The social engineering in Walden Two points to an important area where reconciliation has been difficult when it suggested the elimination of all distinctions in the education process. Our "classes" are simply an application of the human drive to distinguish and classify people and things. Perhaps this has served its purpose, for the need today seems to be that of showing interrelatedness where previously we were content to make distinctions.

2 Forsyth, *Positive Preaching and the Modern Mind*, p. 369.

3 Forsyth, *The Justification of God*, p. 25.

4 Forsyth, *Positive Preaching*, p. 355.

5 We may concede that in the present racial situation in America, the black churches may have no other option than to continue their separate black witness. But racism has to be seen as a *problem* of Christian unity; for if separateness is maintained beyond the point of assuring justice for the black race, it will be another sellout of the gospel for the sake of political power. Let there be no mistake, the white churches bear the weight of guilt for the existence of racism within the church, but the demands of the gospel are equally on us all.

6 *The United Church Herald*, June 1, 1969, pp. 10f.

7 This is developed more fully in *The Church in Search of Its Self*.

8 Cf. *Ministry* (Grand Rapids: Eerdmans, 1966), pp. 70ff.

9 Malcolm Muggeridge, *Jesus Rediscovered*, p. 37.

10 The same fact about ecumenical motivation seems to be true of the attempt to find union in America. The initial moves that led to the establishment of the Consultation on Church Union (COCU) were initiated before the present declining trends began, when the churches were riding high on the crest of influence and popularity. Furthermore, although the ecumenical movement in the 1930s undoubtedly received some impetus from the churches' common struggle against Hitler, it was stimulated at a much more fundamental level in Europe during those years by the theological insights of Karl Barth and a return to biblical theology.

11 Malcolm Muggeridge, *Jesus Rediscovered*, p. 51.

12 P. T. Forsyth, *The Church and the Sacraments*, p. 76.

13 P. T. Forsyth, *Positive Preaching and the Modern Mind*, pp. 22-23.

A POSTSCRIPT

How are we to understand what God is saying in recent events? The year 1973 and the beginning of 1974 destroyed many of the comfortable assumptions we made about our society, our technology and our leadership. In America, the relief many felt about American disengagement from open bloodshed in Southeast Asia rapidly gave way to dismay as the Watergate disgrace seemed to put the whole system of government into question, and the whole sorry story was punctuated by other scandals, which if less distinguished in cast were no less full of high drama and even tragedy for the confidence of the nation. If the highest levels of government were implicated by the fall of a former Vice-President and by Watergate, if the higher echelons of the nation's intelligence services were discredited (the Ellsberg case), business leadership did not look very good (the ITT affair), and some of the labor leadership has not come out of the period smelling any too sweet (the Yablonski murders).

But the unease goes much further, for there is a growing realization that the old stable society of the West is passing away. We are in a totally different world from the one where we enjoyed such a monopoly on the good life and played so happily a few brief years ago —

a world in which political kidnappings, hijackings, terrorism and murders are commonplace, and where extremists have no difficulty in holding innocent people to ransom in full view of a horrified but impotent public. And that which has brought home the change most vividly has been the ease with which the Arab oil powers were able to force the rest of the world to toe the line and pay their price.

What or who is to blame? It would be easy if we could select a convenient scapegoat, and then wash our hands of the whole mess like Pilate. But we cannot do that — not in view of the way in which Western society prodigally used the earth's resources over the past century and chose to mortgage the future of its own children in order to maintain its inflated standards of living; not in view of the injustice it permits within its own boundaries, or of the legalized weaponry it allows to stalk its streets or hoard within its homes; not in view of our casual, corporate indifference to the rest of the world's poverty and need.

"And now God enters the pulpit . . . " It is time for repentance, and for the recognition of his judgment; and for none is repentance more appropriate and more urgent than for those who profess the lordship of Jesus Christ and regularly voice the prayer that his kingdom should be established "on earth as in heaven." For if he *is* the King, how can we fail to see God's judgment in these events?

It is with this conviction that I close this book with a prayer written by Rose-Marie Barth, in the hope that as you read it you will be able to make it your own.

"We are not in high spirits today, Lord. We are not in the mood for jubilation. Our failure to live in your honor and to give glory to you by our labor is more evident than ever. Because of us your name is disgraced among people near and far. Because of us you do not establish your kingdom. For we are concerned with our own security and comfort, not with your will. Daily we despise the bread of life which you would give us.

"We have spread fear not love, oppression not freedom, death not life. For we have forgotten to fear you, Lord. We have abused your kindness, your patience, your mercy. We have cheapened your love and toyed with it as if it were play-money. You have long let us get away with our lies and our greed; you have let us run toward disaster. Now we feel your wrath upon us.

"Under your wrath even the good that we would do brings about evil; even our work for peace and justice brings about strife and scorn. We have no right to appropriate your word of pardon. We fool ourselves by preaching peace and forgiveness as long as your wrath is upon us.

"Wretched creatures that we are! Who will deliver us from your righteous wrath? Can we escape it by fasting, by praying? Even if we perform self-immolation, this would not be the acceptable sacrifice. We are in no position to force your grace. Not even by spiritual violence can we enter your kingdom.

"In our plight we remember your sacrifice, Lord Jesus. Was it not accepted? Were you not raised, are you not alive? Do you not dare us to believe that you are our Savior?

"We do believe. Help our unbelief.

Amen."